ST. JOHN OF DAMASCUS
ON THE DIVINE IMAGES

ST. JOHN OF DAMASCUS

ON THE DIVINE IMAGES

Three Apologies Against Those Who Attack the Divine Images

Translated by

David Anderson

ST. VLADIMIR'S SEMINARY PRESS
CRESTWOOD, NEW YORK 10707
1980

Library of Congress Cataloging-in-Publication Data

Joannes, of Damascus, Saint
   On the divine images.

   1. Icons—Cult—Collected works. 2. Iconoclasm—
Controversial literature—Collected works. I. Title.
BR65.J623P7613   248.3   80-13409
ISBN 0-913836-62-1

Translation © 1980
St. Vladimir's Seminary Press
575 Scarsdale Road
Crestwood, NY 10707-1699

ISBN 0-913836-62-1

Second edition 1994

PRINTED IN THE UNITED STATES OF AMERICA

TABLE OF CONTENTS

INTRODUCTION

The iconoclastic controversy begun in the eighth century by the Byzantine emperor Leo III (717-741) and continued by his successor Constantine V (741-775) cannot be considered in isolation from the Christological controversies of the preceding centuries.[1] Just as earlier ecumenical councils had insisted that the incarnation of Jesus Christ united the second person of the Holy Trinity with human nature, thus making salvation possible by breaking down the wall of separation between God and man, so also the seventh council (787) upheld the doctrine of the veneration of images as an inevitable result of the incarnation. To say that God the Word assumed a human body and soul (and for Him to do so was the only means by which the reign of death and sin in the universe might be destroyed) is to say that the infinite consented to become circumscribed. Therefore, the material flesh of Jesus Christ became part of His divine person, the invisible was made visible, and henceforth it is a good and praiseworthy thing to depict Him as He is: God become man; God become matter. The three treatises of St. John of Damascus all are intended to defend the use and veneration of images as an extension of this most essential of Christian teachings.

St. John of Damascus lived in political isolation from Constantinople. Writing during the reign of Leo III from his monastery of St. Sabbas in a Palestine ruled by the

---

[1] For an historical and theological analysis of the iconoclastic controversy, the reader should refer to J. Meyendorff, *Christ in Eastern Christian Thought*, (St. Vladimir's Seminary Press, 1975), pp. 173-192.

Moslem caliph, he was unhindered by the persecution raging
within the Empire against those who defended the images.
His treatises provide the Orthodox response to the iconoclastic theologians, who based their opposition to the images
on the severe condemnation of idolatry in the Old Testament, as well as an understanding of images as being always
one in essence with their prototypes. Such an understanding
makes every image pretend to be God; therefore every image
is an idol. Furthermore, and most important, the iconoclasts seemed to be little concerned with the historical Jesus
whom the apostles had seen and touched both before and
after His resurrection; instead, they spoke of a divinity whose
assumed humanity was in fact devoid of all uniquely human
characteristics. In this way the iconoclasts dangerously
approached the heresy of Eutyches, who spoke of the humanity of Christ as a mere drop in the ocean of His divinity,
or of Origen, who taught that Christians ought to contemplate God in the purity of their hearts and not use
images from a past that is now over.[2] John of Damascus,
Nicephorus of Constantinople, Theodore the Studite, and
the rest of the defenders of the images saw in these arguments an incomplete understanding of the incarnation, for
by becoming a man, God had entered history, and would
remain part of history until the end of time, and fully human
beyond the end of time.

The crucial argument in the treatises is St. John's con-
tinual insistence that in the incarnation a decisive and
eternal change took place in the relationship between God
and material creation. He says in the first oration, "In
former times, God, being without form or body, could in
no way be represented. But today, since God has appeared
in the flesh and lived among men, I can represent what
is visible in God. I do not worship matter, but I worship
the creator of matter who became matter for my sake. . . ;

[2] See Meyendorff, *op. cit.*, p. 135.

and who, through matter accomplished my salvation. Never will I cease to honor the matter which brought about my salvation!" He accuses those who insist that the Old Testament condemnations of idolatry include all images of quoting Scripture out of context, and then cites passage after passage showing how the same God who forbade the making of idols commanded the use of material objects and images in divine worship and whose temple was adorned with the likenesses of plants and animals which were not worshipped as idols. Each treatise concludes with an extensive selection of patristic passages and historical evidence showing how the use of images had existed in the tradition of the Church for centuries. It is also from Scripture that the treatises derive the indispensable distinction between absolute worship, or adoration (λατρεία) and relative worship, or veneration (προσκύνησις, literally, bowing down before), for the Bible records a great number of incidents where the patriarchs and prophets worship, venerate, and bow before people or places or things to whom such honor is due, but never with the adoration which is given to God alone. He demonstrates that it is wrong to identify every image with its prototype, as the iconoclasts did; rather, the only case when this is so is the Son's relation to the Father as the natural image of the Father; all other images, whether material, symbolical, or allegorical, are essentially different from their prototypes. Thus, the *proskinesis* given by a Christian to an image of Christ is ontologically the same as the reverence he ought to give his fellow Christians, who are also images of Christ, but ontologically different from the *latreia* that is due God alone. In this way St. John warns the iconoclasts that their teaching in effect denies the doctrine of the communion of saints, because if *proskinesis* is forbidden to painted images of God incarnate it must be denied to all other images of Christ as well: the Mother of God, the apostles, and all the saints, who because they have been revealed as faithful

members of Christ's body command the reverence of all
believers. Thus St. John proves that the position of the
iconoclasts begins with an incomplete understanding of
God becoming fully man and ends with a religion so "purified" and "reformed" that it has become disincarnate, a
Manichaeism in which the flesh is not worth saving and
the corporate body of the Church is replaced by the individual's immaterial contemplation of a God who is no longer
Jesus Christ, the Word who became flesh, who was born
of the Virgin, died on the cross, rose from the tomb, and
whose risen Body and Blood is the nourishment of the
faithful in the Eucharistic offering. Iconoclasm, when carried
to its extreme, results in Docetism, where God merely appears to use a body of flesh and then casts it away as so much
dross. Such Docetic iconoclasm is much more than a
problem of the past, for the "popular" or "civil" religion of
our time, which most often is presented as Christianity,
certainly does not revolve around the figure of God incarnate.[3]

A word of explanation is necessary here regarding how
the English words "adoration," "worship," and "veneration"
or "honor" are used in this text. As has already been noted,
St. John of Damascus developed the use of the term *latreia*
to indicate the absolute worship which only God is worthy
by nature to receive, and describes the relative worship
given to the Mother of God, the saints or sacred objects
(books, relics, icons) by the word *proskinesis*. Although
this distinction might appear to be very clear, there are
two complications which might tend to confuse the reader
or translator. First of all, anyone familiar with the Septu-
agint Old Testament (from which these treatises extract
many passages) knows that no such distinction existed at

---

[3] For an edifying fictional portrayal of iconoclasm in the Amer-
ican religious consciousness, see Flannery O'Connor's story "Par-
ker's Back," *The Complete Stories* (Farrar, Strauss, and Giroux,
1976).

the time when the Greek text of the Old Testament was written. *Latreia* was very seldom used and *proskinesis* was used to describe everything from the worship one gives to God to the respect one pays one's friend. Secondly, modern use of English tends to diminish the shades of meaning between words which although they share some similarity are certainly not synonyms. "Adoration," "worship," and "veneration" are regarded by many as synonyms. In order to be consistent with St. John's very exact use of the Greek terms I have in most cases translated *latreia* with "adoration" and *proskinesis* with "veneration" or "honor" or in some cases with the literal verbal rendering "to fall down before." I have not used the word "worship" in such a technical sense; rather it is a generic term of which "adoration" and "veneration" are forms.

It would be a very great mistake to treat the iconoclastic controversy as well as the treatises of St. John as anachronistic curiosities, of interest only to students of Church history. On the contrary, the treatises are written in simple and direct language meant to be easily understood. The errors which St. John fought by his writings are present in our times to an even more alarming extent than when they began. How often is "Christianity" presented solely as an individual's code of ethics, as a "pure" religion not needing the "crutches" of fallen matter; how often is the material placed in direct opposition to the spiritual? The logical result of a disincarnate "Christianity" is the modern "demythologizing" of doctrine which attacks the very core of the Gospel: the preaching of the resurrection of Jesus Christ and the future resurrection and eternal life of all those who believe in Him. St. John's defense of the veneration of images safeguards the witness of the Orthodox Church, that the Jesus of history and the Christ of faith are one and the same, and that division results in turning the Lord into an idea, rather than a person. "Every scribe who has been trained for the kingdom of heaven is like a householder who

brings out of his treasure what is new and what is old."
(Mt. 13:52) St. John's treatises, although old, are always
new since they testify to the eternally new message of the
Gospel, and it is to that end that this translation is dedicated.

The present translation is a thoroughly revised and
amplified version of Mary H. Allies' translation published
in Britain in 1898 by Thomas Baker. I have attempted
to correct errors in the previous translation as well as
eliminate archaic language. I used the Greek text provided
in Volume 94 of Migne's *Patrologia Graeca*; in a few in-
stances a clearer rendering was available from the Latin
text. The only omissions involve a number of the patristic
references which follow the third oration; many of them I
judged to be so repetitious and obscure that I decided to
include a generous sampling which I believe serves the
purpose just as well.

—David Anderson

September, 1979

FIRST APOLOGY OF SAINT JOHN OF DAMASCUS AGAINST THOSE WHO ATTACK THE DIVINE IMAGES

1. Although it is best for us to be ever aware of our unworthiness and to confess our sins before God, nevertheless it is good and necessary to speak when the times demand it, for I see the Church which God founded on the apostles and prophets, her cornerstone being Christ His Son,[1] tossed on an angry sea, beaten by rushing waves, shaken and troubled by the assaults of evil spirits. Impious men seek to rend asunder the seamless robe of Christ and to cut His Body in pieces: His Body, which is the Word of God and the ancient tradition of the Church. Therefore I deem it unreasonable to keep silence and hold my tongue, remembering the warning of Scripture: "If he shrinks back, my soul has no pleasure in him,"[2] and, "If you see the sword coming and do not warn your brother, I shall require his blood at your hand."[3] Fear compels me to speak; the truth is stronger than the might of kings. I heard David, the ancestor of God, singing: "I will speak of Thy testimony before kings, and shall not be put to shame."[4] Therefore I am stirred to speak even more vehemently, for the commanding words of a king must be fearful to his subjects. Yet few men can be found who know enough to despise the evil laws of kings, even though the authority of earthly monarchs does come from above.

2. First of all, I grasp the teaching of the Church,

---

[1] Eph. 2:20.
[2] Heb. 10:38.
[3] Ez. 33:8 (paraph.)
[4] Ps. 119:46.

through which salvation is planted in us, as both foundation
and pillar. I will make the meaning of this teaching evident
because it is both the starting line and the finish line for the
race; it is the bridle of a tightly-reined horse. I see
it to be a great calamity that the Church, progressing in
dazzling superiority and adorned with the highest examples
of the saints of old, should regress to the weak and beggarly
elemental spirits,[5] and be greatly afraid when there is nothing to fear.[6] It is disastrous to suppose that the Church does
not know God as He really is; that she has degenerated into
idolatry, for if she declines one iota from perfection, it
will be a blot on her unblemished face, destroying by its
ugliness the beauty of the whole. A small thing is not small
when it leads to something great; and it is no small matter
to forsake the ancient tradition of the Church which was
upheld by all those who were called before us, whose con-
duct we should observe, and whose faith we should imitate.

3. In the first place before I speak to you, I beg Almighty God before whom all things lie open to bless the
words of my mouth, for He knows my humble purpose and
my sincere intention. May He enable me to bridle my mouth
and direct it to Him and to walk in His straight path, not
turning aside to the right, however convincing it may seem,
or knowing anything about the left. Secondly I ask all God's
people, the holy nation, the royal priesthood, together with
him who has been called to shepherd the flock of Christ's
priesthood in his own person, to receive my treatise with
kindness. They must not dwell on my unworthiness, or ex-
pect eloquence, for I am only too conscious of my short-
comings. Rather, they must consider the power of the
thoughts themselves. The kingdom of heaven does not con-
sist of words, but of deeds. My aim is not to conquer, but
to raise a hand which fights for the truth — a hand which

---

[5] Cf. Gal. 4:9.   [6] Cf. Ps. 52:4 (LXX).

is helped by guidance from Him who is all-powerful. Relying on the invincible truth as my help, I will begin my treatise.

4. I heed the words of Him who cannot deceive: "The Lord our God, the Lord, is one," [7] and, "You shall adore the Lord your God, and worship Him alone," and, "You shall not have strange gods." [8] "You shall not make for yourself a graven image or any likeness of anything that is in heaven above, or that is in the earth beneath," [9] and, "All worshipers of images are put to shame, who make their boast in worthless idols." [10] And again, "The gods who did not make the heavens and the earth shall perish from the earth and from under the heavens." [11] In this way and in a similar manner God spoke in times past to the fathers by the prophets, but last of all in these days He has spoken to us by His only-begotten Son, by whom He made the ages.[12] He says: "This is eternal life, that they know Thee, the only true God, and Jesus Christ, whom Thou hast sent." [13] I believe in one God, the source of all things, without beginning, uncreated, immortal and unassailable, eternal, everlasting, incomprehensible, bodiless, invisible, uncircumscribed, without form. I believe in one superessential Being, one Godhead greater than our conception of divinity, in three persons: Father, Son, and Holy Spirit, and I adore Him alone. I worship one God, one Godhead, but I adore three persons: God the Father, God the Son made flesh, and God the Holy Spirit, one God. I do not adore the creation rather than the Creator, but I adore the one who became a creature, who was formed as I was, who clothed Himself in creation without weakening or departing from His divinity, that He might raise our

---

[7] Deut. 6:4.
[8] Deut. 6:13 (paraph.)
[9] Ex. 20:4.
[10] Ps. 97:7.
[11] Jer. 10:11.
[12] Heb. 1:1-2 (paraph.).
[13] Jn. 17:3.

nature in glory and make us partakers of His divine nature. Together with my King, my God and Father, I worship Him who clothed Himself in the royal purple of my flesh, not as a garment that passes away, or as if the Lord incarnate constituted a fourth person of the Trinity — God forbid! The flesh assumed by Him is made divine and endures after its assumption. Fleshly nature was not lost when it became part of the Godhead, but just as the Word made flesh remained the Word, so also flesh became the Word, yet remained flesh, being united to the person of the Word. Therefore I boldly draw an image of the invisible God, not as invisible, but as having become visible for our sakes by partaking of flesh and blood.[14] I do not draw an image of the immortal Godhead, but I paint the image of God who became visible in the flesh, for if it is impossible to make a representation of a spirit, how much more impossible is it to depict the God who gives life to the spirit?

5. Now some say that God commanded Moses the lawgiver: "You shall worship the Lord your God, and adore Him alone," and, "You shall not make yourself a graven image, or any likeness of anything that is in heaven above, or that is in the earth beneath."

They truly are in error, brothers, for they do not know the Scriptures, that the letter kills, but the Spirit gives life.[15] They do not find in the written word its hidden, spiritual meaning. I can justly say to those people: He who teaches you this will also teach you the following. Listen to the lawgiver's interpretation, which you read in Deuteronomy: "The Lord spoke to you out of the midst of the fire; you heard the sound of words but saw no form; there was only a voice." [16] And shortly thereafter: "Take good heed to yourselves. Since you saw no form on the day that the Lord

---

[14] Cf. Heb. 2:14.   [16] Deut. 4:12.
[15] II Cor. 3:6.   [17] Deut. 4:15-17.

spoke to you at Horeb out of the midst of the fire, beware lest you act corruptly by making a graven image for yourself, in the form of any figure, the likeness of male or female, the likeness of any beast that is on the earth, or the likeness of any bird that flies in the air." [17] And again, "Beware lest you lift up your eyes to heaven, and when you see the sun and the moon and the stars, all the host of heaven, you be drawn away and worship them and serve them." [18]

6. You see that the one thing aimed for is that no created thing can be adored in place of the Creator, nor can adoration be given to any save Him alone. Therefore to worship Him always means to offer Him adoration. For again He says: "You shall have no other gods before Me. You shall not make for yourself a graven image, or any likeness of anything that is in heaven above, or that is on the earth beneath. You shall not worship them or adore them, for I am the Lord your God." [19] And again, "You shall tear down their altars, and dash in pieces their pillars, and burn their Asherim with fire; you shall hew down the graven images of their gods, for you shall not worship other gods." [20] And again, "You shall make for yourself no molten gods." [21]

7. You see that He forbids the making of images because of idolatry, and that it is impossible to make an image of the immeasureable, uncircumscribed, invisible God. For "You heard the sound of words, but saw no form; there was only a voice." [22] This was Paul's testimony as he stood in the midst of the Areopagus: "Being then God's offspring, we ought not to think that the Deity is like gold, or silver, or stone, a representation by the art and imagination of man." [23]

---

[18] Deut. 4:19.
[19] Deut. 5:7-9 (paraph.).
[20] Deut. 12:3.
[21] Ex. 34:17.
[22] Deut. 4:12.
[23] Acts 17:29.

8. These commandments were given to the Jews because of their proneness to idolatry. But to us it is given, on the other hand, as Gregory the Theologian says,[24] to avoid superstitious error and to come to God in the knowledge of the truth; to adore God alone, to enjoy the fullness of divine knowledge, to attain to mature manhood, that we may no longer be children, tossed to and fro and carried about with every wind of doctrine.[25] We are no longer under custodians,[26] but we have received from God the ability to discern what may be represented and what is uncircumscript. "You cannot see My form," [27] the Scripture says. What wisdom the Lawgiver has! How can the invisible be depicted? How does one picture the inconceivable? How can one draw what is limitless, immeasurable, infinite? How can a form be given to the formless? How does one paint the bodiless? How can you describe what is a mystery? It is obvious that when you contemplate God becoming man, then you may depict Him clothed in human form. When the invisible One becomes visible to flesh, you may then draw His likeness. When He who is bodiless and without form, immeasurable in the boundlessness of His own nature, existing in the form of God, empties Himself and takes the form of a servant [28] in substance and in stature and is found in a body of flesh, then you may draw His image and show it to anyone willing to gaze upon it. Depict His wonderful condescension, His birth from the Virgin, His baptism in the Jordan, His transfiguration on Tabor, His sufferings which have freed us from passion, His death, His miracles which are signs of His divine nature, since through divine power He worked them in the flesh. Show His saving cross, the tomb, the resurrection, the ascension into the heavens. Use every kind of drawing, word, or color. Fear not; have

---

[24] *Theological Orations*, 39.
[25] Eph. 4:13-14.
[26] Gal. 3:25.
[27] Cf. Ex. 33:20.
[28] Phil. 2:6-7.

no anxiety; discern between the different kinds of worship. Abraham bowed down to the sons of Hamor, men who had neither faith nor knowledge of God, when he bought the double cave intended to become a tomb.[29] Jacob bowed to the ground before Esau, his brother, and also before the tip of his son Joseph's staff.[30] He bowed down, but he did not adore. Joshua, the son of Nun, and Daniel bowed in veneration before an angel of God,[31] but they did not adore him. For adoration is one thing, and that which is offered in order to honor something of great excellence is another.

9. Since we are speaking of images and worship, let us analyze the exact meaning of each. An image is of like character with its prototype, but with a certain difference. It is not like its archetype in every way. The Son is the living, essential, and precisely similar Image of the invisible God,[32] bearing the entire Father within Himself, equal to Him in all things, except that He is begotten by Him, the Begetter. It is the nature of the Father to cause; the Son is the effect. The Father does not proceed from the Son, but the Son from the Father. The Father who begets is what He is because of His Son, though not in a second place after Him.

10. There are also in God images and models of His acts yet to come: those things which are His will for all eternity, which is always changeless. That which is divine is immutable; there is no variation in Him or shadow due to change.[33] Blessed Dionysius, who has great knowledge of divine things, says that these images and models were marked out before-hand, for in His will, God has prepared all things that are yet to happen, making them unalterable before they come to pass,[34] just as a man who wishes to

---

[29] Gen. 23:7; Acts 7:16.
[30] Gen. 33:3.
[31] Jos. 5:14.
[32] Col. 1:15.
[33] James 1:17.
[34] Cf. *The Divine Names*, Ch. 5.

build a house would first write out a plan and work according to its prescriptions.

11. Again, visible things are corporeal models which provide a vague understanding of intangible things. Holy Scripture describes God and the angels as having descriptive form, and the same blessed Dionysius teaches us why.[35] Anyone would say that our inability immediately to direct our thoughts to contemplation of higher things makes it necessary that familiar everyday media be utilized to give suitable form to what is formless, and make visible what cannot be depicted, so that we are able to construct understandable analogies. If, therefore, the Word of God, in providing for our every need, always presents to us what is intangible by clothing it with form, does it not accomplish this by making an image using what is common to nature and so brings within our reach that for which we long but are unable to see? A certain perception takes place in the brain, prompted by the bodily senses, which is then transmitted to the faculties of discernment, and adds to the treasury of knowledge something that was not there before. The eloquent Gregory says that the mind which is determined to ignore corporeal things will find itself weakened and frustrated.[36] Since the creation of the world the invisible things of God are clearly seen [37] by means of images. We see images in the creation which, although they are only dim lights, still remind us of God. For instance, when we speak of the holy and eternal Trinity, we use the images of the sun, light, and burning rays; or a running fountain; or an overflowing river; or the mind, speech, and spirit within us; or a rose tree, a flower, and a sweet fragrance.

12. Again, an image foreshadows something that is

---

[35] Cf. *On the Celestial Hierarchies*, Ch. 1.
[36] *Theological Orations*, 2.   [37] Rom. 1:20.

yet to happen, something hidden in riddles and shadows. For instance, the ark of the covenant is an image of the Holy Virgin and Theotokos, as are the rod of Aaron and the jar of manna. The brazen serpent typifies the cross and Him who healed the evil bite of the serpent by hanging on it. Baptismal grace is signified by the cloud and the waters of the sea.[38]

13.   Again, things which have already taken place are remembered by means of images, whether for the purpose of inspiring wonder, or honor, or shame, or to encourage those who look upon them to practice good and avoid evil. These images are of two kinds: either they are words written in books, as when God had the law engraved on tablets and desired the lives of holy men to be recorded, or else they are material images, such as the jar of manna, or Aaron's staff,[39] which were to be kept in the ark as a memorial. So when we record events and good deeds of the past, we use images. Either remove these images altogether, and reject the authority of Him who commanded them to be made, or else accept them in the manner and with the esteem which they deserve. In speaking of the proper manner, let us consider the question of worship.

14.   Worship is the means by which we show reverence and honor. Let us understand that there are different degrees of worship. First of all there is adoration, which we offer to God, who alone by nature is worthy to be worshipped. Then, for the sake of Him who is by nature to be worshipped, we honor His friends and companions, as Joshua, the son of Nun, and Daniel bowed in worship before an angel, or as David venerated God's holy places, when he says, "Let us go to His dwelling place; let us worship at His footstool," [40] or as when the people of Israel once offered

---

[38] I Cor. 10:1.   [39] Ex. 34:28; Heb. 9:4.   [40] Ps. 132:7.

sacrifices and worshipped in His tent, or encircled the
temple in Jerusalem, fixing their gaze upon it from all sides
and worshipping as their kings had commanded, or as Jacob
bowed to the ground before Esau, his elder brother,[41] and
before Pharaoh, the ruler whose authority was established
by God.[42] Joseph's brothers prostrated themselves in homage on the ground before him.[43] Other worship is
given to show respect, as was the case with Abraham and
the sons of Nahor.[44] Either do away with worship com-
pletely, or else accept it in the manner and with the esteem
it deserves.

15. Answer me this question: "Is there one God?" You
will answer, Yes, I assume there is only one Lawgiver.
What? Does He then command contrary things? The
cherubim are not outside creation. How can He allow
cherubim, carved by the hands of men, to overshadow the
mercy-seat? Is it not obvious that since it is impossible
to make an image of God, who is uncircumscribed and unable to be represented, or of anything like God, creation
is not to be worshipped and adored as God? But He allows
the image of cherubim who are circumscribed, to be made
and shown as prostrate in adoration before the divine
throne, overshadowing the mercy-seat, for it was fitting that
the image of the heavenly servants should overshadow the
image of the divine mysteries. Would you say that the ark,
or the staff, or the mercy-seat, were not made by hands?
Are they not the handiwork of men? Do they not owe their
existence to what you call contemptible matter? What is the
meeting-tent itself, if not an image? Was it not a type, a
figure? Well then, listen to the holy apostle's words concerning those things that are of the law! "They serve as
a copy and shadow of the heavenly sanctuary, for when
Moses was about to erect the tent, he was instructed by

---

[41] Gen. 33:3.   [42] Gen. 47:7.   [43] Gen. 50:18.   [44] Gen. 23:7.

God saying, 'See that you make everything according to the pattern which was shown you on the mountain.' "[45] But the law was not an image, but the shadow of an image, for as the same apostle says: "For since the law has but a shadow of the good things to come instead of the true form of the realities . . ." [46] If the law forbids images, and yet is itself the forerunner of images, what shall we say? If the meeting tent was a shadow and the image of an image, how can it be true that the law does not forbid the making of images? But this is not at all the case, for there is a season for everything; a time for every matter under heaven.[47]

16. In former times God, who is without form or body, could never be depicted. But now when God is seen in the flesh conversing with men,[48] I make an image of the God whom I see. I do not worship matter; I worship the Creator of matter who became matter for my sake, who willed to take His abode in matter; who worked out my salvation through matter. Never will I cease honoring the matter which wrought my salvation! I honor it, but not as God. How could God be born out of things which have no existence in themselves? God's body is God because it is joined to His person by a union which shall never pass away. The divine nature remains the same; the flesh created in time is quickened by a reason-endowed soul. Because of this I salute all remaining matter with reverence, because God has filled it with His grace and power. Through it my salvation has come to me. Was not the thrice-happy and thrice-blessed wood of the cross matter? Was not the holy and exalted mountain of Calvary matter? What of the life-bearing rock, the holy and life-giving tomb, the fountain of our resurrection, was it not matter? Is not the ink in the most holy Gospel-book matter? Is not the life-giving altar

---

[45] Heb. 8:5; Ex. 25:40.   [47] Eccl. 3:1.
[46] Heb. 10:1.   [48] Bar. 3:38.

made of matter? From it we receive the bread of life! Are
not gold and silver matter? From them we make crosses,
patens, chalices! And over and above all these things, is
not the Body and Blood of our Lord matter? Either do away
with the honor and veneration these things deserve, or
accept the tradition of the Church and the veneration of
images. Reverence God and His friends; follow the inspira-
tion of the Holy Spirit. Do not despise matter, for it is not
despicable. God has made nothing despicable. To think such
things is Manichaeism. Only that which does not have its
source in God is despicable—that which is our own invention,
our willful choice to disregard the law of God—namely, sin.
If you despise and abhor the command to make images
because they are material things, consider the words of
Scripture: "And the Lord said to Moses: See, I have called
by name Bezalel the son of Uri, son of Aur, of the tribe
of Judah, and I have filled him with the spirit of God with
ability and intelligence, with knowledge and all craftsman-
ship to devise artistic designs, to work in gold, silver and
bronze, in cutting stones for setting and in carving wood,
for work in every craft. And behold, I have appointed with
him Oholiab, the son of Ahisamach, of the tribe of Dan,
and I have given ability to all able men, that they may make
all that I have commanded you." [49] And again, "Moses said
to all the congregation of the people of Israel: This is the
thing which the Lord has commanded. Take from among
you an offering to the Lord; whoever is of a generous heart,
let him bring the Lord's offering: gold, silver, and bronze;
blue and purple and scarlet stuff and fine twined linen;
goats' hair, tanned rams' skins and goatskins; acacia wood,
oil for the light, spices for the anointing oil and for the
fragrant incense, and onyx stones and stones for setting, for
the ephod and for the breastplate. And let every able man
among you come and make all that the Lord has com-

[49] Ex. 31:1-6.

manded, the tabernacle, etc." [50] Behold the glorification of matter, which you despise! What is more insignificant than colored goatskins? Are not blue and purple and scarlet merely colors? Behold the handiwork of men becoming the likeness of the cherubim! How can you make the law a reason for refusing to do what the law itself commands? If you invoke the law in your despising of images, you might just as well insist on keeping the sabbath and practicing circumcision. But it is certain that "if you receive circumcision, Christ will be of no advantage to you. I testify again to every man that if he receive circumcision, he is bound to keep the whole law. You are severed from Christ, you who would be justified by the law; you have fallen away from grace." [51] Israel of old did not see God, but "we all, with unveiled face, behold the glory of the Lord." [52]

17. We use all our senses to produce worthy images of Him, and we sanctify the noblest of the senses, which is that of sight. For just as words edify the ear, so also the image stimulates the eye. What the book is to the literate, the image is to the illiterate. Just as words speak to the ear, so the image speaks to the sight; it brings us understanding. For this reason God ordered the ark to be constucted of wood which would not decay, and to be gilded outside and in, and for the tablets to be placed inside, with Aaron's staff and the golden urn containing the manna, in order to provide a remembrance of the past, and an image of the future. Who can say that these were not images, heralds sounding from far off? They were not placed aside in the meeting-tent, but were brought forth in the sight of all the people, who gazed upon them and used them to offer praise and worship to God. Obviously they were not adored for their own sake, but through them the people were led to remember the wonders of old and to worship God, the

---

[50] Ex. 35:4-10.   [51] Gal. 5:2-4.   [52] II Cor. 3:18.

worker of wonders. They were images serving as memorials;
they were not divine, but led to the remembrance of divine
power.

18. God ordered twelve stones to be taken from the
Jordan, and specified why, for He says: "When your children
ask their fathers in time to come, what do these stones
mean? Then you shall let your children know, Israel passed
over this Jordan on dry ground, for the Lord your God
dried up the waters of the Jordan for you until you passed
over," [53] and thus the ark was saved and all the people.
Shall we not then record with images the saving passion and
miracles of Christ our God, so that when my son asks me,
"What is this?" I may say that God the Word became man,
and that through him not only Israel passed through the
Jordan, but the whole human race regained its original hap-
piness? Through Him, human nature rose from the lowest
depths to the most exalted heights, and in Him sat on the
Father's throne.

19. Some would say: Make an image of Christ and of
His Mother, the Theotokos, and let that be enough. What
foolishness! Your own impious words prove that you utterly despise the saints. If you make an image of Christ,
and not of the saints, it is evident that you do not forbid
images, but refuse to honor the saints. You make images
of Christ as one who is glorified, yet you deprive the saints
of their rightful glory, and call truth falsehood. The Lord
says, "I will glorify those who glorify me." [54] The divinely-
inspired apostle writes, "So through God you are no longer
a slave but a son, and if a son, then an heir." [55] And "if
children, then heirs, heirs of God and fellow heirs with
Christ, provided we suffer with Him in order that we may
also be glorified with Him." [56] You are not waging war

---

[55] Gal. 4:7.   [53] Jos. 4:21-22.   [54] I Sam. 2:30.   [56] Rom. 8:17.

against images, but against the saints themselves. St. John
the Theologian, who leaned on the breast of Christ, says
"We shall become like Him." [57] Just as something in con-
tact with fire becomes fire not by its own nature, but by
being united, burned, and mingled with fire, so it is also,
I say, with the assumed flesh of the Son of God. By union
with His person, that flesh participates in the divine nature
and by this communion becomes unchangeably God; not
only by the operation of divine grace, as was the case with
the prophets, but by the coming of grace Himself. The
Scripture calls the saints gods, when it says, "God has taken
His place in the divine council; in the midst of the gods
He holds judgment." [58] St. Gregory interprets these words
to mean that God takes His place in the assembly of the
saints, determining the glory due each.[59] The saints during
their earthly lives were filled with the Holy Spirit, and when
they fulfill their course, the grace of the Holy Spirit does not
depart from their souls or their bodies in the tombs, or
from their likenesses and holy images, not by the nature
of these things, but by grace and power.

20.   God told David that through his son a temple
would be built, and that His resting-place would be prepared. As the Books of Kings tell us, Solomon, while he
was building the temple, also made the cherubim. "And he
overlaid the cherubim with gold and carved all the walls
of the house round about with carved figures of cherubim
and palm trees and open flowers, in the inner and outer
rooms." [60] Is it not even better to adorn the Lord's house
with holy forms and images, instead of beasts and plants?
What has become of this law which declares "You shall
make for yourself no graven image?" Solomon was given
the gift of wisdom, and built the temple, the image of
heaven. He made the likenesses of bulls and lions, which

[57] I Jn. 3:2.   [58] Ps. 82:1.   [59] *Theological Orations*, 40.

the law forbade. Now if we make images of Christ, and
images of the saints, which are filled with the Holy Spirit,
will they not increase our reverence? Just as the people and
the temple were once purified by the blood of goats and
bulls and the sprinkling of a heifer's ashes,[61] so we are
cleansed by Christ, who in His testimony before Pontius
Pilate made the good confession,[62] and who is Himself the
example of martyrs. He builds His Church on the foundation of the blood of the saints. There the forms of lifeless
beasts adorned the temple; here we use living and reasonable
images.

21. We depict Christ as our King and Lord, then, and
do not strip Him of His army. For the saints are the Lord's
army. If the earthly emperor wishes to deprive the Lord
of His army, let him also dismiss his own troops. If he
wishes in his tyranny to refuse due honor to these valiant
conquerors of evil, let him also cast aside his own purple.
For if the saints are heirs of God and co-heirs with Christ,[63]
they will also share in the divine glory and dominion. If
they have partaken of Christ's sufferings, and are His
friends, shall they not receive a share of glory from the
Church on earth? "No longer do I call you servants," God
says, "but I have called you friends."[64] Shall we strip them
of the glory given them by the Church? What audacity!
What effrontery of mind, to fight with God, refusing to
follow His commands! You who refuse to bow before images
also refuse to bow before the Son of God who is the living
image of the invisible God,[65] and His unchanging likeness.
I bow before the images of Christ, the incarnate God; of
our Lady, the Theotokos and Mother of the Son of God;
and of the saints, who are God's friends. In struggling
against evil they have shed their blood; they have imitated

---

[60] I Kgs. 6:28-29.   [62] I Tim. 6:13.   [64] Jn. 15:15.
[61] Heb. 9:13.   [63] Rom. 8:17.   [65] Col. 1:15.

Christ who shed His Blood for them by shedding their blood
for Him. I make a written record of the prowess and sufferings of those who have walked in His footsteps, that I may
be sanctified, and be set on fire to imitate them zealously.
St. Basil says, "the honor given to the image is transferred
to its prototype." [66] If you build churches to honor the saints
of God, then make images of them as well. The temple of
old was not built in the name of any man, nor was the death
of the righteous an occasion for feasting, but rather for
tears. He who touched a corpse was considered unclean,[67]
even if the corpse was Moses himself. But now the memory
of the saints is kept with rejoicing. There was weeping at
the death of Jacob, but there was joy at the death of Stephen.
Therefore either give up the joyful feasts of the saints, since
they are not part of the old law, or accept the images which
you say are contrary to the law. But it is impossible not to
keep the memory of the saints with rejoicing, for the choir
of holy apostles and God-bearing fathers insist that we
do so. From the time that God the Word became flesh,
He is like us in everything except sin, and partakes of our
nature without mingling or confusion. He has deified our
flesh forever, and has sanctified us by surrendering His
Godhead to our flesh without confusion. And from the
time that God, the Son of God, who is unchangeable by
reason of His Godhead, chose to suffer voluntarily, He
wiped out our debt, by paying for us a most admirable and
precious ransom. We are all made free through the blood
of the Son, which pleads for us to the Father, and by His
descent into the grave, when He went and preached to the
souls imprisoned there for many ages,[68] and gave freedom
to the captives, sight to the blind,[69] and bound the strong
one.[70] He rose by the excellence of His power, keeping the

---

[66] *Letters on the Holy Spirit*, 18.
[67] Num. 19:11.   [69] Is. 61:2.
[68] I Pet. 3:19.   [70] Mt. 12:29.

immortal flesh by which He had saved us from corruption. And from the time when we were born again of water and the Spirit, we have become sons of God and members of His household. For this reason St. Paul calls the faithful saints.[71] Therefore we do not grieve but rejoice over the death of the saints. We are not under the law but under grace,[72] having been justified by faith,[73] and having seen the one true God. For the law is not laid down for the just,[74] nor do we serve as children, held under the law,[75] but we have reached the estate of mature manhood, and are fed on solid food, not on that which leads to idolatry. The law was good, as a lamp shining in a dark place until the day dawns, and the morning star rose in our hearts.[76] The living water of divine knowledge has driven away pagan seas, and now all may know God. The old creation has passed away, and all things are made new.[77] The holy apostle Paul said to Peter the prince of the apostles: "If you, though a Jew, live like a Gentile and not like a Jew, how can you compel the Gentiles to live like Jews?" [78] And he writes to the Galatians: "I testify again to every man who receives circumcision that he is bound to keep the whole law." [79]

22. Of old, those who did not know God were in bondage to beings that by nature are no gods.[80] But now that we have come to know God, or rather to be known by Him, how can anyone turn back again to the weak and beggarly elemental spirits, and be their slaves once more? [81] For I have seen God in human form, and my soul has been saved. I gaze upon the image of God, as Jacob did,[82] but in a different way. For he only saw with spiritual sight what was promised to come in the future, while the memory of

---

[71] I Cor. 1:2ff.
[72] Rom. 6:14.
[73] Rom. 5:1.
[74] I Tim. 1:9.
[75] Gal. 4:1ff.
[76] Cf. II Pet. 1:19.
[77] II Cor. 5:17.
[78] Gal. 2:14.
[79] Gal. 5:3.
[80] Gal. 4:8.
[81] Gal. 4:9.
[82] Gen. 32:30.

Him who became visible in the flesh is burned into my soul. Peter's shadow, or handkerchiefs and aprons carried from Paul's body, healed the sick and put demons to flight.[83] Shall the paintings and images of the saints not be glorified? Either refuse to worship any matter, or stop your innovations. Do not remove age-old boundaries, erected by your fathers.[84]

23. The tradition of the Church is not only passed on in written documents, but has also been given in unwritten form. In chapter twenty-seven of St. Basil's book of thirty chapters written to Amphilochius concerning the Holy Spirit, he says "Among the carefully guarded teachings and doctrines of the Church, there are some teachings we received from written documents, while others we receive secretly, for they have been handed on to us from the apostolic tradition. Both sources have equal power to lead us to righteousness. No one who values the seasoned discipline of the Church will dispute with this, for if we neglect unwritten customs as not having much force, we then bury much of the Gospel which is vitally important." Those are the words of Basil the Great. How then can we know anything about the holy place of Calvary or the life-giving tomb? Is not such unwritten information handed down from father to sons? For it is written that the Lord was crucified at the place of the skull, and buried in a tomb which was hewn out of a rock by Joseph; [85] but it is from unwritten tradition that we know the locations of these places, and worship there now. There are other examples. What is the origin of the three immersions at baptism, or praying toward the east, or the manner in which we celebrate the eucharist? Therefore the holy apostle Paul says: "So then, brethren, stand firm and hold to the traditions which you were taught by us, either by word of mouth or

---

[83] Acts 5:15.   [84] Prov. 22:28.   [85] Mt. 27:60.

by letter." [86] Therefore, since so much that is unwritten has
been handed down in the Church and is still observed now,
why do you despise images?

24. If you speak of pagan abuses, these abuses do not
make our veneration of images loathsome. Blame the
pagans, who made images into gods! Just because the
pagans used them in a foul way, that is no reason to object
to our pious practice. Sorcerers and magicians use incantations and the Church prays over catechumens; the former
conjure up demons while the Church calls upon God to exorcise the demons. Pagans make images of demons which
they address as gods, but we make images of God incarnate,
and of his servants and friends, and with them we drive
away the demonic hosts.

25. If you object that the great St. Epiphanius utterly forbade images, in the first place the writing in question
is fictitious and inauthentic. It is the work of someone who
used Epiphanius' name, which is a common enough practice. Secondly, we know that the blessed Athanasius ob-
jected to the relics of the saints being put into chests, and
that he preferred them to be buried in the earth, wishing
to abolish the disgusting custom of the Egyptians, who did
not bury their dead under the earth, but displayed them on
beds and couches. Let us suppose that the great Epiphanius
really wrote this work, wishing to correct a similar abuse
by forbidding the making of images. Even so, the proof
that he did not object to them is found in his own church,
which we see adorned with images to this very day. Thirdly,
one exception cannot be a law for the Church, nor does a
single swallow's song mean that spring has come to stay,
as Gregory, the theologian and teacher of truth, says.[87]
Nor can a single opinion overturn the unanimous tradition

---

[86] II Thess. 2:15.   [87] *Theological Orations*, 38.

of the whole Church, which has spread to the ends of the earth.

26. Accept, therefore, the teaching of the Scriptures and the fathers. If the Scripture says, "The idols of the nations are silver and gold, the work of men's hands," [88] it is not forbidden to bow before inanimate things, or the handiwork of men, but only before those images which are the devil's work.

27. We have seen that prophets bowed before angels, and men, and kings, and those who knew not God, and even a staff. David says, ". . . and worship at His footstool." [89] Isaiah, speaking in God's name, says, "Heaven is my throne and the earth is my footstool." [90] It is obvious to all that the heavens and the earth are created things. Moses, Aaron, and all the people worshipped before things made with hands. Paul, the golden voice of the Church, says in the Epistle to the Hebrews, "But when Christ appeared as a high priest of the good things to come, then He entered once for all through the greater and more perfect tent, not made with hands, a type of the true one, but into heaven itself." [91] Thus the former holy things, the tent, and everything therein were made by hands, and no one can deny that they were venerated.

---

[88] Ps. 135:15.   [90] Is. 66:1.
[89] Ps. 99:5.   [91] Heb. 9:11, 24.

ANCIENT DOCUMENTATION AND TESTIMONY OF THE HOLY FATHERS CONCERNING IMAGES

St. Dionysius the Areopagite, *The Letter to Titus:*

... And instead of attacking the common understanding of them (i.e., images), we ought to comprehend their sacred significance, and not despise their divine origin or the sacred things which they portray, for they are visible manifestations of hidden and marvellous wonders.

Commentary: See that he warns us not to despise the honorable images.

The same, from Chapter 1 of *The Divine Names:*

... through the sacred veils of the Scriptures and ecclesiastical traditions which explain spiritual truths with terms drawn from the sensual world, and super-essential truths in terms drawn from nature, clothing with shapes and forms things which are shapeless and formless, and by a variety of different symbols fashioning manifold attributes of the immaterial and supernatural simplicity.

Commentary: If it is good for men to clothe with shape and form according to our understanding that which is shapeless, formless, and simple, shall we then not make forms and images of things which are visible and perceptible to us, that we may remember them, and so be moved to imitate them?

The same, from Chapter 1 of *The Ecclesiastical Hierarchy:*

... but if the ranks and essences above us, which we have already reverently mentioned, are without bodies, then their hierarchy is above material understanding. But we supply a variety of symbols, using things we see and com-

*prehend, and so we are led by natural things to the divine
simplicity of God and His goodness. Bodiless spirits form
their own spiritual perceptions, but we are led to the perception of God and His majesty by visible images.*

Commentary: If it is reasonable that we are led to the
understanding of divine and immaterial things by using
material images, and if God in His providence and love for
mankind clothes in form and image what is without form
or image for our sake, what is wrong with making perceptible images of Him who in His love for mankind stooped
down to assume our form and shape?

An esteemed tradition has been handed down to us
from the beginning that Abgar, the King of Edessa, was
set on fire with divine love by hearing of the Lord, and sent
messengers asking Him to visit him. But if this request
were declined, they were ordered to have His likeness painted. Then He, who is all-knowing and omnipotent, is said
to have taken a piece of cloth and pressed it to His face,
impressing upon it the image of His countenance, which it
retains to this day.

St. Basil the Great, from his sermon on the blessed
martyr Barlaam, which begins "In the first place, the death
of the saints . . .":

*Now, arise, you renowned painters of the champions'
brave deeds, who by your exalted art make images of the
General. My praise of the crowned champion is dull compared with the wisdom which inspires your brush with
its radiant colors. I will refrain from writing further of the
martyr's valor, for you have crowned him and I rejoice
today at the victory won by your power. As I look at the
detail in your painting of his struggle, I see his hand among
the flames; your image has made his victory even more
brilliant for me. Let the demons be enraged, for they are
struck down by the goodness of the martyr, which you have
depicted. May his hand, burned in the flames of old, again
be revealed as victorious. Would that I may be included*

*in this image, and be united with Christ, the Judge of the
contest. To Him be glory unto ages of ages. Amen.*

The same from the *Thirty Chapters to Amphilochius on
the Holy Spirit*, from Chapter 18:

*The image of the emperor is also called the emperor,
yet there are not two emperors. Power is not divided, nor
is glory separated. Just as He who rules us is one power,
so the homage He receives from us is united, not divided,
for the honor given to the image is transferred to the prototype. Therefore, the One whom the image materially represents is He who is Son by nature. Just as the likeness
of a corresponding form is made by the artists, so also in
the divine and unconfused nature, union is accomplished
by divine indwelling.*

Commentary: If the image of the king is the king, and
the image of Christ is Christ, and the image of a saint is
the saint, and if power is not divided or glory separated,
then the honor given to an image is given to the one portrayed in the image. Devils are in fear of the saints, and flee
from their shadow. A shadow is an image; therefore I make
images to terrify the demons. If you say that only intellectual worship is worthy of God, then take away all corporeal things: lights, the fragrance of incense, prayer made
with the voice. Do away with the divine mysteries which
are fulfilled through matter: bread, wine, the oil of chrism,
the sign of the cross. All these things are matter! Take away
the cross and the sponge of the crucifixion, and the spear
which pierced His lifegiving side. Either give up honoring
all these things, or do not refuse to honor images. Matter
is filled with divine grace through prayer addressed to those
portrayed in images. Purple cloth by itself is a simple thing,
and so is silk, and a cloak is woven from both. But if the
king should put it on, the cloak receives honor from the
honor given to him who wears it. It is the same with matter.
By itself it deserves no worship, but if someone portrayed
in an image is full of grace, we become partakers of the

grace according to the measure of our faith. The apostles
saw the Lord with bodily eyes; others saw the apostles, and
others the martyrs. I too desire to see them both spiritually
and physically and receive the remedy by which the ills
of both soul and body (for I am composed of both) may be
healed. What I see with my eyes I venerate, but not as
God; I revere that which portrays what I honor. You, perhaps, are superior to me, and have risen so far above bodily
things that you have become virtually immaterial and feel
free to make light of all visible things, but since I am human
and clothed with a body, I desire to see and be present with
the saints physically. Condescend from your heights to my
lowly state of mind, for by doing so you will make your
lofty position safe. God accepts my longing for Him and
for His saints. The Master rejoices when His servants are
rewarded with praise, as Basil declares in his panegyric for
the Forty Holy Martyrs. Listen to what he says in honor
of the martyr Gordius.

From the sermon of St. Basil on the martyr Gordius:

*The people rejoice with spiritual joy at the memory of
those who accomplished righteous deeds; when they hear
of such holiness, they are urged to imitate it zealously. For
the history of holy men lights the way for those who would
follow the path of salvation. And again, whenever we re-
count the lives of those who excelled in righteousness, we
glorify in the first place the Master of those servants and
then we praise the servants, on account of the testimony
we know them to have borne, while the people are filled
with joy when they hear of such goodness.*

Commentary: You see that praising the saints glorifies
God; the memory of the saints brings joy and salvation to
the people. Why do you wish to destroy it? This remembrance is accomplished through sermons and images, as
the same holy Basil says.

From the same on the martyr Gordius:

Just as light comes from fire and fragrance from myrrh,

so it must be also that benefit follows the practice of good deeds. It is no small thing accurately to record the edifying events of the past. Was it a faint memory of the man's brave struggle that was preserved and given to us? How do the painter's images seem to resemble it? Whenever images are copied from other images, it is likely that most of them will depart from the prototype. But since we shun these dangers, there is little hazard that we have diminished the truth.

The same, at the end of the sermon:

When we see the sun, we are always filled with wonder. So also when we have his memory before our eyes, it will always remain fresh.

Commentary: Obviously sermons and images are the best means of keeping it fresh.

The same, from his sermon on the Forty Holy Martyrs:

Can the lover of the martyrs ever have enough of their memory? The honor given to the righteous, our fellow servants, is a testimony of the goodwill of our common Master.

And again:

Bless the marytrs heartily, that you may be a martyr by intention. Thus, even though you depart this life without persecutor, fire, or lash, you will still be found worthy of the same reward.

Commentary: How, then, could you ever dissuade me from honoring the saints. Are you jealous of my salvation?

Listen to what he says further on, comparing the art of the painter to preaching:

When we expound on their memory in the midst of all we make them helpful for the living, showing the holiness of these men for an example to all, as in a picture.

Commentary: Do you understand that both images and sermon serve the same purpose? He says, "Let us show them forth in a sermon, as in a picture." And again he says this:

Both painters of words and painters of pictures illustrate valor in battle; the former by the art of rhetoric;

the latter by clever use of the brush, and both encourage everyone to be brave. A spoken account edifies the ear, while a silent picture induces imitation.

Commentary: What more conspicuous proof do we need that images are the books of the illiterate, the never silent heralds of the honor due the saints, teaching without use of words those who gaze upon them, and sanctifying the sense of sight? Suppose I have few books, or little leisure for reading, but walk into the spiritual hospital — that is to say, a church — with my soul choking from the prickles of thorny thoughts, and thus afflicted I see before me the brilliance of the icon. I am refreshed as if in a verdant meadow, and thus my soul is led to glorify God. I marvel at the martyr's endurance, at the crown he won, and inflamed with burning zeal I fall down to worship God through His martyr, and so receive salvation. Have you not heard the same holy father, at the beginning of his sermon on the Psalms, when he says that "the Holy Spirit, knowing that the race of men is lazy regarding righteousness and stubborn to follow leadership, set the psalms to tuneful music." What do you say to this? Shall I not bear witness to the martyr both by word and paintbrush? Shall I not embrace with my eyes that which is a wonder to the angels and to all creation; painful to the devil and the terror of demons, as the same great light of the Church has said? And again, he says near the end of his panegyric on the Forty Holy Martyrs: "O holy choir! O sacred brotherhood! O unbroken rank of shields! Guards in common of the human race! Communion of goodness! Helpers of your petitioners! Most powerful intercessors! Stars of the inhabited world, flowers of the Church! Flowers, I say both spiritual and material. Though the earth never covered you, the heavens received you, opening to you the gates of paradise. Truly you are a spectacle worthy of the angelic army, worthy of the patriarchs, the prophets, and the righteous."

Commentary: Shall I not long to see the desire of the

angels? Basil's brother Gregory the bishop of Nyssa, who is of one mind with him, says the following:

From St. Gregory, Bishop of Nyssa, from the supplement to *The Structure of Man:*

According to the ways of men those who make images of rulers make an impression of the form and clothe what they have made with the dignity of royal purple, and are accustomed to call such an image the king. So it is with human nature. Since it was fashioned to rule over others, it was created as a living image, to be in communion with the name and dignity of its archetype.

The same, from the fifth chapter of the same work:

The beauty of divinity cannot be pictured with beautiful forms or bold colors, but is perceived in unutterable blessedness, in virtue of its excellence. Therefore human forms are what painters transfer to the canvas using various colors, adding suitable and harmonious tints to the image, trying with precision to capture in the image the beauty of its archetype.

Commentary: You see that the beauty of divinity cannot be pictured with beautiful forms, and therefore no image can be made of it; it is human form which is transferred to the canvas by the artist's colors. Therefore if the Son of God assumed the form of man taking the form of a servant, and coming in man's likeness, why should His image not be made? If according to common parlance the honor due the image is transferred to the prototype, as holy Basil says, why should we not bow down to honor the image, not as God, but as the image of God incarnate?

The same, from his sermon at Constantinople on the divinity of the Son and the Spirit, and on Abraham:

Then the father proceeds to bind his son. I have often seen paintings of this touching scene, and could not refrain from shedding tears, so vivid was the scene reproduced by the artist. Isaac is lying on the altar, his legs bound, his hands tied behind his back. The father approaches the victim, clasps his hair with his left hand, stoops over the face so pitifully turned towards him, and holds the knife in his right hand ready to strike. The point of the knife is already on the body when the divine voice is heard, forbidding him to kill his son.

St. John Chrysostom, from his sermon on the Epistle to the Hebrews:

How can what comes first be the image of what is to follow, as Melchizedek is of Christ? Melchizedek is used as an image in the Scriptures in the same way as a silhouette is an outline for a portrait. Because of this, the law is called a shadow, and grace and truth are what is foreshadowed. Consequently, the law personified by Melchizedek is a silhouette of Him whose portrait, when it appears, is grace and truth inscribed in the body. So the Old Testament is a silhouette of things to come in a future age, while the New Testament is the portrait of those things.

Leo, Bishop of Neapolis in Cyprus, from his book *Against the Jews,* on the veneration of the cross of Christ, and the images of the saints, and on the relics of the saints:

If you, O Jew, reproach me by saying that I worship the wood of the cross as I worship God, why do you not reproach Jacob for bowing down before the point of Joseph's staff? It is obvious that he was not worshipping wood, but that he was bowing before Joseph by means of the wood. So with us; we glorify Christ through the cross, and not the wood itself.

Commentary: If we bow down before the cross, no matter what substance it is made from, shall we not bow down before the image of Him who was crucified upon it?

From the same:

Abraham did homage to the faithless men who sold him the cave which became a tomb, and bowed his knee to the ground, but he did not worship them as gods. Jacob blessed Pharaoh, who was an impious idolater, but he did not bless him as God. Again, he bowed down to the ground at Esau's feet, yet did not worship him as God. Does not God order us to bow down before the earth and mountains? "Extol the Lord our God, and worship at His holy mountain, and bow down before His footstool, for He is holy." [92] *The earth is his footstool, for he says "Heaven is my throne and earth is my footstool."* [93] *How could it be that Moses worshipped Jethro who was an idolater,* [94] *and Daniel worshipped the impious Nebuchadnezzar? How can you reproach me for honoring those who honor and worship God? Tell me, is it more suitable to honor the saints, or to throw stones at them, as you do? Is it not fitting to venerate them, rather than to saw your benefactors in pieces and fling them into the mud? If you loved God, you would be eager to show honor to His servants also. And if the bones of righteous men are unclean, why were the bones of Jacob and Joseph brought with all honor from Egypt?* [95] *How was it that a dead man immediately rose when the bones of Elisha were touched to him?* [96] *If God works wonders through bones, it is obvious that by His power He can also work them through images, stones, and many other things, as was the case when Elisha gave his staff to his servant and said, "Go, lay my staff upon the face of the Shunamite woman's son."* [97] *With his staff Moses rebuked Pharaoh, parted the waters, and made them return to their courses, and struck the rock so that water gushed forth. Solomon said, "Blessed is the wood by which justice comes."* [98] *Elisha threw a stick into the Jordan, and drew out the iron axe-head.* [99] *This wood typified nothing other than the wood of life, the tree of forgiveness. Moses lifted the bronze serpent on a wooden pole, and gave life to the people.* [100] *The blossoming rod in the meeting-tent confirmed Aaron's priesthood.* [101] *Perhaps*

---

[92] Ps. 99:9,5.   [95] Gen. 50:5ff, Ex. 13:19.   [98] Wis. 14:7.
[93] Is. 66:1.   [96] II Kgs. 13:21.   [99] II Kgs. 6:4-7.
[94] Ex. 18:7.   [97] II Kgs. 4:29.   [100] Num. 21:9.
[101] Num. 17:8.

you will say to me, O Jew, that God commanded before-
hand to Moses concerning everything that was to be put in
the tent of the testimony, but I reply to you that Solomon
had a great variety of things made for the temple in carving
and sculpture, which God had not enjoined him to make.[102]
These things were not placed in the tent of the testimony,
nor did Ezekiel see them in the vision God showed him
of the temple,[103] *but Solomon brought no condemnation upon*
himself by doing this. He had these images made for the
glory of God, just as we do. You had many distinct signs
and images to help you remember God, but through your
ingratitude you have lost them. For instance, you had the
rod of Moses, the tables of the law, the burning bush, the
rock that gushed with water, the jar of manna, the fire from
God that came down upon the altar, the plate inscribed
with the divine name, the God-given ephod, the tent over-
shadowed by God. If you had fashioned all these things by
day and by night, saying, "Glory be to Thee, the only Al-
mighty God, for Thou hast done wonders in Israel through
all these things," if you would have carried out all these
ordinances of the law and fallen down to worship God, you
would see that worship has always been given to Him by
use of images.

And further on:

If you sincerely love your friend, or your king, or es-
pecially your benefactor, if you should see his son or his
servant, do you not embrace him, or if you see his staff
or his throne, or his crown, or his house, do you not salute
them? If you thus honor a benefactor or the emperor, how
much greater should be the honor you give to God! Again
I say, Would that you had made images according to the
law of Moses and the prophets, and each day worshipped
the God and Master who commanded them. Therefore
when you see Christians bowing down before the cross,
know that they bow down to Christ crucified, and not to
the wood. If, indeed, they paid such honor to wood as wood,

they would be bound to worship trees of every kind, as you did of old, O Israel, saying to the tree and to the stone, "You are my father, or you gave me birth." [104] *We do not address the cross or the images of the saints in this way. They are not our gods, but are like books which lie open in the churches in the sight of all. We venerate them, and thus are reminded of the honor we owe God. He who honors the martyr honors God to whom the martyr bore witness; he who venerates the apostle of Christ worships Him who sent the apostle. He who falls at the feet of Christ's mother most certainly gives honor to her Son. There is no God but one: He who is known and adored in Trinity.*

Commentary: Who is the faithful interpreter of blessed Epiphanius' words? Leontius, whose teachings have adorned the island of Cyprus, or those who speak according to their own hearts? Listen to the words of Severianus, Bishop of Gabala.

From the sermon of Severianus, Bishop of Gabala, on the Dedication of the Church of Our Savior:

How could the image of the enemy bring life to our ancestors? And again he says, How could the image of the enemy bring salvation to the distressed people? Would it not have been more reasonable to say, "If anyone among you is bitten, look up to heaven, where God is on high, and you shall be saved," or "Look towards God's tabernacle." But he did not say anything like that, but sets up the image of the cross alone. Why did Moses do such a thing? He had already said to the people, "You shall not make for yourselves a graven image, or any likeness of anything that is in heaven above, or that is in the earth beneath, or that is in the water under the earth." [105] *But how shall I speak to the arrogant? Tell me, devout servant of God, will you do what is forbidden, or will you ignore what you have been*

---

[102] II Chron. 3:1ff.   [104] Jer. 2:27.
[103] Ez. 40:47ff.   [105] Ex. 20:4.

commanded to do? He who said, "You shall not make for yourselves a graven image," who condemned the golden calf, now makes a bronze serpent, and not in secret, but openly, so that it is known to all. Moses would answer that this commandment was given to root out material impiety and to keep all the people safe from apostasy and idolatry, but now I cast a bronze serpent for a good purpose — to prefigure the truth. And just as I have erected the tabernacle and everything in it, and the cherubim, which are likenesses of what is invisible to hover over the holy place, as a shadow and a figure of what is to come, so also I have set up a serpent for the salvation of the people, as an endeavor to prepare them for the image of the sign of the cross, and the salvation and redemption which it brings. As a sure confirmation of this, listen to the Lord's own word: "As Moses lifted up the serpent in the wilderness, so must the Son of man be lifted up that whoever believes in Him may have eternal life." [106]

Commentary: Notice that the commandment not to make images was given to lead the people away from idolatry, to which they were prone, but the serpent lifted on high was an image of our Lord's sufferings. Listen to what I say, for the making of images is no new invention, but is an ancient practice known to the most holy and eminent of the fathers. Helladius, the disciple of blessed Basil and successor to his episcopal see, says that the holy man was standing by an icon of our Lady, on which was painted the image of Mercurius, the renowned martyr, praying for the removal of the godless tyrant Julian the Apostate, and received a revelation from the icon. He saw the martyr vanish for a short time, and then reappear, holding a spear which he was preparing to throw.

Taken word for word from the life of St. John Chrysostom:

---

[106] Jn. 3:14.

Blessed John loved the epistles of the wise Paul very much . . . he had an icon of the holy apostle, which he kept in a place where he would occasionally go to rest because of his bodily infirmities. It was his nature to keep many vigils. And while he read St. Paul's epistles he would gaze intently at the image, and would hold it as if it were alive, and bless it, and direct his thoughts to it, as though the apostle himself were present and could speak to him through the image . . . When Proclus finished speaking, he gazed intently at the icon of the apostle Paul, and recognized it to be the image of the man he had seen conversing with John. He reverenced John, pointing to the icon and saying, Forgive me, Father, but he whom I saw speaking to you looks like this. In fact, I should think he is the same.

In the life of righteous Eupraxia, it is written that her superior showed her an image of the Lord.

It is written in the life of St. Mary of Egypt that she prayed before the icon of our Lady, begging her intercession, and by doing so was able to enter the church.

St. Sophronius, the archbishop of Jerusalem, from his book *The Spiritual Garden:*

The abbot Theodore Aeliotes used to tell this story: Once there was a hermit on the Mount of Olives who was engaged in spiritual warfare, and a demon of lust fought with him. At one time, while the demon tormented him vehemently, the elder struggled to maintain his self-control, and in tears said to the demon, "For how much longer will you not show yourself to me? Either depart from me at once, or stand up to me and fight!" The demon appeared visibly to him and said, "Swear to me that you will tell no one what I have to tell you and I will torment you no longer." And the elder swore by Him who dwells on high, "I will tell no man what you say to me." Then the demon said to him, "Bow down before that image no more, and I will torment you no longer." For he had an icon there, a figure of our Lady the Holy Theotokos Mary, who gave

*birth to our Lord Jesus Christ. The hermit said to the demon,
"I know you! Depart from me!" Then on the next day he
came to the abbot Theodore Aeliotes, who lived in the
Pharon monastery, and told him everything. And the abbot
said to the hermit, "You have been deceived because you
swore to a demon. Nevertheless, if you do what I say, all
will be well. It will be profitable for you if you never again
allow this lust to enter into that place, which would have you
refuse to worship our Lord and God Jesus Christ together
with His own Mother." Then he stood fast, strengthened
by those excellent words, and departed to that same place.
And again the demon appeared to the hermit, and said to
him, "What is within you, miserable old man? Did you not
swear to me, that you would tell no one? How is it that
you have told everything to him that came to you? I tell
you, miserable old man, you will be judged for swearing
falsely on the day of judgement!" And the hermit answered
him saying, "If I swore, I swore falsely, and I was aware
of it, but I will not listen to you ever again."*

Commentary: You see that we must bow down before
the image of her who is portrayed, and how great an evil it
is to refuse veneration, and how even the demon of lust
is aware of this, for it would have pleased the demon more
if the old man ceased honoring the icon, than if he com-
mited the sin of impurity.

Among all the Christian kings and priests, the wise and
the pious, renowned by their words and their lives, in all
the councils of the holy and inspired fathers, have these
things not been pointed out? We are not inventing a new
faith. "For the law shall go forth out of Zion," the Holy
Spirit said prophetically, "and the word of the Lord from
Jerusalem." [107] We do not advocate one thing at one time
and change it at another; otherwise the faith would become
a joke to those outside. We will not allow an imperial edict

---

[107] Is. 2:3.

to overturn the body of teachings handed down from the fathers. It is not for would-be pious kings to overthrow the boundaries of the Church. This is not the fathers' way; it is piracy to impose things by force, and they do not bear credence.

What happened during the second council of Ephesus bears witness to this, when an unjust decree was forced through by the emperor's hand, and blessed Flavian was put to death. What do emperors have to do with councils? The Lord says, "where two or three are gathered in my name, there am I in the midst of them." [108] Christ did not give to kings the power to bind and to loose, but to the apostles,[109] and to the pastors and teachers who succeed them. St. Paul says, "But even if . . . an angel from heaven should preach to you a gospel contrary to that which we preached to you . . ." [110] but we will be silent about what follows,[111] hoping for their conversion. But if we see that they ignore the warning — may the Lord forbid it! — we will make use of the rest. Let us hope it will not be necessary.

If anyone should enter a house and see painted on the walls a pictorial history of Moses and Pharaoh, he might ask, "Who are those who walk across the sea as if it were dry land?" Would you not answer, "They are the sons of Israel." "Who is dividing the sea with his rod?" Would you not say, "Moses?" So if someone makes an image of Christ crucified, and you are asked who He is, would you not reply, "It is Christ God, who became incarnate for us?" Yes, Master, we worship all that is of You; inflamed with love for You we embrace Your divinity, Your power, Your goodness, Your mercy towards us, Your condescension, Your incarnation. And just as we would shrink back before red-hot iron, not because of the nature of iron but because of the fiery heat, so we worship Your flesh, not because of

---

[108] Mt. 18:20.   [110] Gal. 1:8.
[109] Mt. 18:18.   [111] I.e. "Let them be anathema!"

its fleshly nature, but because it is inseparably united to Your divine person. We worship Your sufferings. Who has ever heard of death being worshipped, or suffering honored? Yet we truly worship our God's physical death and His saving sufferings. We venerate Your image; we bow down before anything that is concerned with You; Your servants, Your friends, and most of all Your Mother, the Theotokos.

We beseech the people of God, the holy nation, to hold fast to the tradition of the Church. Even a small erosion of what has been handed down to us would undermine the foundation-stones, and in a very short time would overthrow the entire house. May we prove to be steadfast, unbending, immovable, founded on the strong rock who is Christ, to whom be glory, honor, and worship, with the Father and the Holy Spirit, now and ever and unto the endless ages of ages. Amen.

SECOND APOLOGY OF ST. JOHN OF DAMASCUS
AGAINST THOSE WHO ATTACK
THE DIVINE IMAGES

1. I ask your forgiveness, my masters, and I beg you to receive my words, for I offer them in sincerity, though I am the least profitable servant of God's Church. It is not any vision of my own glory that has moved me to speak — may God be my witness — but zeal for the truth. Only in this do I place my hope of salvation and so with trust I go to meet Christ my Master, expecting and praying that He will receive it as a sacrificial offering for the remission of my shameful transgressions. The man who had received five talents from his master acquired five more, and likewise the man with two acquired two more. He who received one and buried it, returning it without even interest, was indeed a wicked servant, and banished to the outer darkness.[1] Fearing lest the same fate should befall me, I yield to the Master's commands, and using the gift of words He has given me, I set before you a table laden with wisdom, so that when my Lord comes He may find that I have multiplied the fruit of souls, and having shown myself a faithful servant He may receive me into His sweetness and joy, for which I long. Give me ears willing to hear; open to me the altars of your hearts. Receive my treatise; sincerely ponder the power of my arguments. This is the second part of my work concerning images. Certain children of the Church have urged me to write it because the first treatise was not sufficiently clear to all. Therefore be indulgent with me, as I fulfill my promise.

---

[1] Mt. 25:20ff.

2. The author of evil, beloved, the jealous serpent of old — I mean the devil — wages war in many ways against man who was created in God's image, and as the result of his opposition, death came into the world. From the very beginning he filled man with the lust to become like God and through that covetousness he dragged man down to share the death of beasts. And this is not all, for he often tempts man with shameful and brutish pleasures. What a contrast between wishing to become a god and shameful lusts! And again, he led men to become faithless, as David, the ancestor of God says so well, "The fool says in his heart, there is no God." [2] Sometimes he brought men to worship many gods; at other times, he turned them away from the true God to worship demons, or else the heavens and the earth, or the sun, the moon, the stars, and the rest of creation, or even wild beasts and reptiles, for it is as bad to refuse to give honor when honor is due, as to give glory where it is not deserved. Again, he has taught some to call the uncreated God evil, and has deceived others to profess that God, who is by nature good, is the author of evil; some he has deceived by the misconception that if there is one nature in the Godhead, there can be only one person, or if there are three persons, then there must be three natures; or if our Lord Jesus Christ is one person, then He can have but one nature, or if He has two natures, then He is two persons.

3. But the truth keeps us in the middle of the road, utterly denying these absurdities and teaching us to confess one God who is one nature and three persons: Father, Son, and Holy Spirit. Evil is not a substance, but an accident: [3] that which opposes a thought, or a word, or an action to God's law, having its origin in the thought or

---

[2] Ps. 14:1.
[3] St. John here uses Aristotelian terms to describe evil.

word or action. When any of these come to an end, so also the evil ceases to exist. The truth also proclaims that in Christ, who is one of the Holy Trinity, there are two natures and one Person.

4. Now the devil, who is the enemy of the truth and fights against the salvation of mankind, in suggesting that images of corruptible man, or birds, or beasts, or reptiles should be made and worshipped as gods, led not only the Gentiles astray, but also many of the children of Israel.[4] Now, in these days, he is eager to disturb the peace of Christ's Church through false lips and treacherous tongues which use God's word for an evil purpose, attempting to disguise his shameful and dark intention, luring the hearts of the weak away from the true patristic usage. Some have risen up saying that it is wrong to make and display images of the saving wonders of Christ and the struggles of the saints against the devil, that by gazing upon them we may be moved to wonder, and glorify God. Is there anyone having knowledge of divine matters and spiritual sense that does not perceive in this a deception of the devil? For he does not wish to be conquered, and to have his shame exposed to all, or the glory of God and of His saints to be proclaimed in public.

5. If we attempted to make an image of the invisible God, this would be sinful indeed. It is impossible to portray one who is without body: invisible, uncircumscribed, and without form. Again, if we made images of men and believed them to be gods, and adored them as if they were so, we would be truly impious. We do neither of these things. But we are not mistaken if we make the image of God incarnate, who was seen on earth in the flesh, associated with men, and in His unspeakable goodness assumed

---

[4] Rom. 1:23.

the nature, feeling, form, and color of our flesh. For we yearn to see how He looked, as the apostle says, "Now we see through a glass darkly." [5] Now the icon is also a dark glass, fashioned according to the limitations of our physical nature. Though the mind wear itself out with effort, it can never cast away its bodily nature.

6. Shame on you, wicked devil, for grudging us the sight of our Master's likeness, and the holiness which proceeds from it. You would prevent us from gazing upon His saving sufferings, marvelling at His condescension and praising His Almighty power. You are jealous of the honor which God has given to the saints. You wish us neither to see their glory portrayed nor zealously to imitate their courage and faith. We will not follow your suggestions, O wicked devil, hater of mankind! Listen, you peoples, nations, and languages, you men, women and children, elders, young men and infants, and all the holy Christian people. If anyone should preach to you something contrary to what the catholic Church has received from the holy apostles, fathers, and councils, and has guarded to this present day, do not listen to him. Do not receive advice from a serpent, as Eve did, and receive death. If an angel or an emperor teaches you anything contrary to what you have received, close your ears. The holy apostle said instead of "close your ears," *let him be anathema.*[6] Thus far I have refrained from saying this, for I hope for their amendment.

7. Those who do not understand the mind of Scripture say that God said through Moses the lawgiver: "You shall not make for yourself a graven image, or any likeness of anything that is in heaven above, or that is in the earth beneath." [7] And that He said through David the prophet: "All worshipers of images are put to shame, who make their

---

[5] I Cor. 13:12.   [6] Gal. 1:8.   [7] Ex. 20:4.

boast in worthless idols," [8] and many similar things. Whether they quote from the divine Scriptures or the holy fathers, it is always with this same intention. How shall we reply to this? How else, if not with the words our Lord spoke to the Jews: "Search the Scriptures." [9] It is good to search the Scriptures, but we must attend to them with a discerning mind. Beloved, it is impossible that God should prove false.[10] There is one God, one Lawgiver of the Old and New Testaments, who "spoke of old in many and various ways to our fathers by the prophets, but in these last days He has spoken to us through His (only-begotten) Son." [11] Now use your mind with precision. It is not I who am speaking, but the Holy Spirit who declares plainly through the holy apostle Paul, "God spoke of old in many and various ways to our fathers by the prophets." Note that God spoke *in many and various ways*. A skillful doctor does not prescribe the same for all alike, but for each according to his need, taking into consideration the sickness and the climate, season and age, giving one kind of medicine to a child, another to a grown man, according to his age, one thing to a weak patient, another to a strong, and to each sufferer the right thing for his condition and ailment: one thing in the summer, another in the winter, another in the spring or autumn, using what is most suitable in each place. In the same way the most excellent physician of souls prescribed correctly for those who were still children and susceptible to the sickness of idolatry, holding idols to be gods, and worshipping them as such, abandoning the worship of God, offering to the creature the glory due the Creator. He commanded them not to do this. It is impossible to make an image of God, who is bodiless, invisible, immaterial, without form, uncircumscribed, and who cannot be touched. How can we portray what is invisible? "No one has ever seen God; the

---

8 Ps. 97:7.   10 Heb. 6:18.
9 Jn. 5:39.   11 Heb. 1:1.

only God, who is in the bosom of the Father, He has made Him known." [12] And again, "You cannot see My face; for man shall not see Me and live." [13]

8. There is no doubt that they worshipped idols as gods. Listen to what Scripture says concerning the Exodus of the sons of Israel, when Moses ascended Mt. Sinai to pray for a time. While he was receiving the law, the stiff-necked people rose up and said to Aaron, the servant of God: "Make us gods who shall go before us; as for this Moses, the man who brought us up out of Egypt, we do not know what has become of him." [14] Then, when they had looked over their wives' trinkets, and made the calf, they ate and drank, and drunk with wine and madness, they made merry, saying in their folly, "These are your gods, O Israel." Do you not see that they worshipped idols, which are the abode of demons, as gods, and that they adored creatures instead of the Creator? As the divine apostle says, "They exchanged the glory of the immortal God for images resembling mortal man or birds or animals or reptiles, and served the creature rather than the Creator." [15] For this reason God forbade them to make any image, as Moses says in the book of Deuteronomy: "Then the Lord spoke to you, and out of the midst of the fire you heard the sound of words, but saw no form; there was only a voice." [16] And again, "Take heed, and keep your soul diligently. Since you saw no form on the day that the Lord spoke to you at Horeb out of the midst of the fire, beware lest you act corruptly by making a graven image for yourselves, in the form of any figure, the likeness of male or female, the likeness of any beast that is on the earth, the likeness of any winged bird that flies in the air." [17] And

---

[12] Jn. 1:18.
[13] Ex. 33:20.
[14] Ex. 32:1ff.

[15] Rom. 1:23, 25.
[16] Deut. 4:12.
[17] Deut. 4:9, 15-17.

again, "And beware lest you lift up your eyes to heaven, and when you see the sun and the moon and the stars, all the host of heaven, you be drawn away and worship them and serve them . . ." [18] You see that the one object is that the creature be not adored in place of the Creator, and that adoration should be given to none but the Creator alone. In every case he is speaking of adoration. Again, "You shall have no other gods before Me; you shall not make for yourself a graven image, or any likeness . . ." [19] Again, "You shall make for yourself no molten gods." [20] You see that He forbids the making of images because of idolatry and that it is impossible to make an image of the bodiless, invisible, and uncircumscribed God. "You saw no form on the day that the Lord spoke . . ." [21] and St. Paul, standing in the midst of the Areopagus, says: "Being therefore God's offspring, we ought not to think that the Deity is like gold, or silver, or stone, a representation by the art and imagination of man." [22]

9. You have heard what is said: "You shall not make for yourself a graven image, or any likeness." Now listen to what is added: "You shall make a veil (for the tabernacle of the testimony) of blue and purple and scarlet stuff and finely twined linen; in skilled work shall it be made, with cherubim." [23] And, "He made a mercy seat of pure gold . . . and he made two cherubim of hammered gold." [24] How do you explain this, O Moses? On the one hand you say, "You shall not make for yourself a graven image, or any likeness," and yet you yourself have cherubim woven on the veil and two cherubim fashioned of pure gold. But listen to what the answer of God's servant Moses might be: "O blind and stupid people, listen to the force of these

---

[18] Deut. 4:19.   [21] Deut 4:15.   [24] Ex. 37:6-7.
[19] Deut. 5:7.   [22] Acts 17:29.
[20] Ex. 34:17.   [23] Ex. 26:31.

words, and guard your souls carefully. Yes, I said that since you saw no form on the day that the Lord spoke to you at Horeb out of the midst of the fire, beware lest you act corruptly by making a graven image for yourselves; you shall not make for yourselves molten gods. I did not say, You shall not make images of cherubim, which spread out their wings overshadowing the mercy seat. What I did say was, You shall not make for yourselves molten gods, and, You shall not make for yourself any likeness; you shall not bow down to them and serve them as God, nor shall you adore the creature instead of the Creator. You shall have no other gods before Me; you shall adore no creature as God; you shall not adore the creature instead of the Creator."

10. See how the purpose of Scripture is made clear to those who search for it intelligently. For you must know, beloved, that truth must be distinguished from falsehood in everything, and it is necessary to investigate whether the motive of each deed is good or bad. For in the Gospels we find that all things, whether good or evil, are mentioned: God, the angels, man, heaven, earth, water, fire, air, sun, moon, stars, light, darkness, Satan, demons, serpents, scorpions, death, hell, virtues and vices. And because everything spoken concerning all of them is true and the purpose of the Gospels is to glorify God and the saints whom He has glorified, to lead us to salvation and purification, that the devil and his demons may be cast down, we bow before them, we embrace and love them, we kiss them with our eyes, our lips, our hearts, and similarly all the rest of the Old and New Testaments, and the words of the holy and elect Fathers. But we cast off in abhorrence the foul, loathsome, and unclean writings of the accursed Manichaeans, Gnostics, and the rest of the heretics as containing nothing but vanities and lies, giving glory to the devil and his demons and bringing them joy, even though

they are full of God's name. But concerning this business
of images, we must search for the truth, and the intention
of those who make them. If it is really and truly for the
glory of God and of His saints, to promote virtue, the
avoidance of evil, and the salvation of souls, then accept
them with due honor, as images, remembrances, likenesses
and books for the illiterate. Embrace them with the eyes,
the lips, the heart; bow before them; love them, for they
are likenesses of God incarnate, of His mother, and of the
communion of saints, who shared the sufferings and the
glory of Christ, who conquered and overthrew the devil,
his angels, and his deceit.

11. If anyone should dare to make an image of the
immaterial, bodiless, invisible, formless, and colorless Godhead, we reject it as a falsehood. If anyone should make
images to give glory, honor, and worship to the devil and
his demons, we abhor them and deliver them to the flames.
Or if anyone makes idols of men, birds, reptiles, or any
creature, we anathematize him. Just as the holy fathers
pulled down the temples and altars of the demons, and
raised churches on the same spot which they named for
the saints whom we honor, so also they threw down the
images of demons, and instead raised up the images of
Christ, the Theotokos, and the saints. Even under the old
dispensation, Israel never built temples named for men or
celebrated the memory of men. The human race was under
the curse, and death was the condemnation, and the source
of grief. A corpse was reasoned to be unclean; likewise
anyone who touched it. But since divine nature has assumed
our nature, we have been given a life-bearing and saving
remedy, which has glorified our nature and led it to in-
corruption. Therefore we celebrate the death of the saints;
churches are built in their honor, and their icons are painted.
But be assured that if any man sets his hand to throw
down an image set up as a memorial to glorify Christ, His

Mother the holy Theotokos, or any of the saints, an image
which shames the devil and his consorts, an image which
was made with godly desire and zeal, and will not bow
down to honor and embrace the image as he should (but
not as God), that man is an enemy of Christ, the holy
Theotokos, and the saints, and an advocate of the devil and
his crew, for by his action he reveals his vexation that God
and His saints are honored and glorified and the devil put
to shame. The icon is a hymn of triumph, a manifestation,
a memorial inscribed for those who have fought and conquered, humbling the demons and putting them to flight.

12. What right have emperors to style themselves
lawgivers in the Church? What does the holy apostle say?
"And God has appointed in the church first apostles, second
prophets, third teachers and shepherds, for building up
the body of Christ." [25] He does not mention emperors. And
again, "Obey your leaders and submit to them; for they
are keeping watch over your souls, as men who will have
to give account." [26] And again, "Remember your leaders,
those who spoke to you the word of God; consider the
outcome of their life, and imitate their faith." [27] Emperors
have not preached the word to you, but apostles and prophets, shepherds and teachers. When God gave commands
to David concerning the house David intended to build for
Him, He said to him, "You may not build a house for my
name, for you are a warrior and have shed blood." [28] "Pay
all of them their dues," the apostle Paul says, "taxes to
whom taxes are due, revenue to whom revenue is due,
respect to whom respect is due, honor to whom honor is
due." [29] Political prosperity is the business of emperors;
the condition of the Church is the concern of shepherds and

---

[25] I Cor. 12:28.   [28] I Chron. 28:3.
[26] Heb. 13:17.   [29] Rom. 13:7.
[27] Heb. 13:7.

teachers. Any other method is piracy, brothers. Saul rent Samuel's cloak, and what was the consequence? God tore the kingdom away from him, and gave it to David the meek.[30] Jezebel pursued Elijah, who escaped her clutches, but the day came when pigs and dogs would lick up her blood, and her body would be trampled by horses.[31] Herod killed John, but worms ate Herod.[32] And in our own day blessed Germanus, a shining example by his words and deeds, is punished with exile, and with him how many more bishops and fathers whose names are unknown? Is this not piracy? When the Scribes and Pharisees surrounded our Lord, supposedly to listen to His teaching, and questioned Him, "Is it lawful to pay taxes to Caesar, or not?" He answered them, "Bring me a coin." And when they had brought it He said, "Whose likeness and inscription is this?" They said, "Caesar's." Then He said to them, "Render therefore to Caesar the things that are Caesar's, and to God the things that are God's." [33] We will obey you, O emperor, in those matters which pertain to our daily lives: payments, taxes, tributes; these are your due and we will give them to you. But as far as the government of the Church is concerned, we have our pastors, and they have preached the word to us; we have those who interpret the ordinances of the Church. We will not remove the age-old landmarks which our fathers have set,[34] but we keep the tradition we have received. For if we begin to erode the foundations of the Church even a little, in no time at all the whole edifice will fall to the ground.

13. You despise matter, and call it contemptible. So did the Manichaeans, but the divine Scriptures proclaim it good, for it says, "And God saw everything that he had made, and behold, it was very good." [35] Therefore I declare

---

[30] I Sam. 15:27-28.
[31] I Kgs. 19:2, 3; II Kgs. 9:33ff.
[32] Acts 12:23.
[33] Mt. 22:17ff.
[34] Prov. 22:28.
[35] Gen. 2:31.

that matter is the creation of God, and a good thing. But if you say that it is bad, you are either saying that it does not come from God, or else you make God the origin of all evil. Listen to what the divine Scriptures say concerning matter, which you despise: "Moses said to all the congregation of the people of Israel, This is the thing which the Lord has commanded. Take from among you an offering to the Lord; whoever is of a generous heart, let him bring the Lord's offering: gold, silver, and bronze; blue and purple and scarlet stuff and fine twined linen; goats' hair, tanned rams' skins, and goatskins; acacia wood, oil for the light, spices for the anointing oil and for the fragrant incense, and onyx stones and stones for setting, for the ephod and for the breastpiece. And let every able man among you come and make all that the Lord has commanded." [36]

14. Behold, the glorification of matter, which you despise! What is more insignificant than colored goatskins? Are not blue and purple and scarlet merely colors? Behold the handiwork of men becoming the likeness of the cherubim! Was not the meeting-tent an image in every way? "And see that you make them after the pattern for them, which is being shown you on the mountain." [37] Yet all the people stood around it and worshipped! Were not the cherubim kept where all the people could see them? Did not the people gaze upon the ark, and the lampstand, and the table, the golden urn and Aaron's rod, and fall down in worship? I do not worship matter; I worship the Creator of matter, who became matter for me, taking up His abode in matter, and accomplishing my salvation through matter. "And the Word became flesh and dwelt among us." [38] It is obvious to everyone that flesh is matter, and that it is created. I salute matter and I approach it with reverence, and I worship that through which my salvation has come.

---

[36] Ex. 35:4-10.   [37] Ex. 25:40.   [38] Jn. 1:14.

I honor it, not as God, but because it is full of divine grace
and strength. If you reject images because of the law, why
is it that you do not keep the sabbath, and practice circumcision, for the law unyieldingly commands these things. You
must observe all the law and not celebrate the Lord's pass-
over from Jerusalem. But understand that if you keep the
law Christ will be of no advantage to you.[39] It is time for
you to take your brother's wife in marriage, and raise up
seed to your brother,[40] and not sing the song of the Lord in
a foreign land.[41] But enough of this! "You are severed from
Christ, you who would be justified by the law; you have
fallen away from grace." [42]

15. The temple which Solomon built was dedicated
with the blood of animals, and decorated with the images
of animals: lions and oxen, and palm trees and pome-
granates. Now the Church is consecrated by the blood of
Christ and His saints, and it is adorned with the images
of Christ and the saints. Either do away with the worship
of images altogether, or do not be an innovator, "removing
the age-old boundaries erected by your fathers." [43] I am not
talking about those things which were established before
the coming in the flesh of Christ our God, but about that
which has come to pass after His sojourning among us. For
God Himself finds fault with the commandments of the
Old Testament, for He says, "I gave them statutes that
were not good and ordinances by which they could not have
life," [44] because of their hardness of heart. "For when there
is a change in the priesthood, there is necessarily a change
in the law as well." [45]

16. The eye-witnesses and ministers of the Word

---

[39] Gal. 5:2.   [42] Gal. 5:4.   [44] Ez. 20:25.
[40] Deut. 25:5ff.   [43] Prov. 22:28.   [45] Heb. 7:12.
[41] Ps. 137:4.

handed down ecclesiastical ordinances not only in written form, but also by unwritten tradition. Why do we bow before the cross? Has not unwritten tradition instructed us concerning these things? Therefore the holy apostle Paul says, "So then, brethren, stand firm and hold to the traditions which you were taught by us, either by word of mouth or by letter." [46] Therefore, since so much that is not written has been handed down in the Church and is still observed now, why do you despise images? The Manichaeans wrote the Gospel according to Thomas; will you now write the Gospel according to Leo? I will not permit a tyrannical emperor to plunder priestly concerns. The emperor has received no power to bind and loose. I know of the emperor Valens, supposedly a Christian, who persecuted the Orthodox faith. I know of Zeno and Anastasius, Heraclius and Constantine of Sicily, who was called Bardanes Philippicus. I will not believe that Church order is drawn up by imperial edicts, but by the traditions of the fathers, both written and unwritten. Just as the written Gospel has been preached to the whole world, so also there has been an unwritten tradition throughout the world to make icons of Christ, the incarnate God, and of the saints, to bow down before the cross, and to pray facing the east.

17. If you speak of pagan abuses, these abuses do not make our veneration of images loathsome. Blame the pagans who made images into gods! Just because the pagans used them in a foul way, that is no reason to object to our pious practice. Sorcerers and magicians use incantations; so also the Church prays over catechumens; the former conjure up demons, while the Church calls upon God to exorcise the demons. Pagans sacrificed to demons; Israel offered blood and fat to God. The Church offers the bloodless sacrifice to God. Pagans make images into demons, and

[46] II Thess. 2:15.

Israel made images into gods, for they said, "These are
your gods, O Israel, who brought you up out of the land
of Egypt."[47] But we have set up images of the true God, who
became incarnate, and of His servants and friends, and
with them we drive away the demonic hosts.

18. If you say that blessed Epiphanius clearly forbade us to have images, know that these words attributed
to him are spurious, and were written by someone using
Epiphanius' name, as has happened often. A father does
not fight his own offspring. For all have become partakers
of the one Holy Spirit. The Church has borne testimony
to this by adorning herself with images, until some have
risen up against this practice, throwing Christ's flock into
confusion, polluting the waters from which the people of
God drink.

19. If I honor and venerate the cross, the lance, the
reed, or the sponge, by which the murderers of God mocked
and murdered my Lord, shall I not also bow before
images made by believers with good intentions, who wish
to glorify and keep in remembrance the sufferings of Christ?
If I bow before the image of the cross, regardless of what
kind of matter has been used to make it, shall I not venerate
the image of the Crucified One, who won our salvation on
the cross? What outrageous inhumanity! Obviously I do
not worship matter; for if it should happen that a cross,
which has been fashioned from matter, should be ruined,
I would consign it to the fire, and the same with damaged
images.

20. Receive as a single stream the testimony of
Scripture and the fathers; it shows you that the making
and worship of images is no new invention, but the ancient
tradition of the Church. In the holy gospel according to
Matthew, the Lord calls His own disciples blessed, and with

them everyone who conforms to their example, following
in their footsteps. He says: "Blessed are your eyes, for they
see, and your ears, for they hear. Truly, I say to you, many
prophets and righteous men longed to see what you see, and
did not see it, and to hear what you hear, and did not hear
it." [48] We also long to see what is possible for us to see.
"Now we see in a mirror dimly," [49] in the image, and thus
we are blessed. God Himself first made an image, and presented images to our sight, for "God created (the first) man
in His own image,"[50] and Abraham, Moses, Isaiah, and all
the prophets saw images of God, but not the essence of
God. The burning bush was an image of God's Mother,
and when Moses was about to approach it, God said, "Do
not come near; put off your shoes from your feet, for the
place on which you are standing is holy ground." [51] Now
if the ground where Moses saw an image of the Theotokos
is holy ground, how much more holy is the image itself?
Not only is it holy, I daresay, but the holy of holies. When
the Pharisees asked the Lord, "Why then did Moses command one to give a certificate of divorce, and to put her
away?" [52] he answered, "For your hardness of heart Moses
allowed you to divorce your wives, but from the beginning
it was not so." [53] And I tell you that Moses, knowing the
sons of Israel to be hard-hearted and seeing that they easily
fell into idolatry, forbade them to make images. But we are
not the same, for we stand firmly on the rock of faith, filled
with the light of divine knowledge.

21. Hear the words of the Lord: "You blind fools!
He who swears by the temple, swears by it and by Him who
dwells in it; and he who swears by heaven swears by the
throne of God and by Him who sits upon it." [54] And he

---

[47] Ex. 32:4.   [50] Gen. 1:27.   [53] Mt. 19:8.
[48] Mt. 13:16-17.   [51] Ex. 3:5.   [54] Mt. 23:21-22.
[49] I Cor. 13:12.   [52] Mt. 19:7.

who swears by an image, swears by the one the image represents.

22. It has been sufficiently demonstrated that the tent, the veil, the ark, the altar, and everything within the tent, were images and types, the works of men's hands, and that they were venerated by all Israel, and that the carved cherubim were also made by God's command. For God said to Moses, "And see that you make them after the pattern for them, which is being shown you on the mountain." [55] Listen also to the testimony of the apostle Paul, that Israel bowed before images and human handiwork, by God's command: "Now if He were on earth He would not be a priest at all, since there are priests who offer gifts according to the law. They serve a copy and shadow of the heavenly sanctuary, for when Moses was about to erect the tent, he was instructed by God saying, 'See that you make everything according to the pattern which was shown you on the mountain.' But as it is, Christ has obtained a ministry which is as much more excellent than the old as the covenant He mediates is better, since it is enacted on better promises. For if that first covenant had been faultless, there would have been no occasion for a second. For He finds fault with them when He says, 'The days will come, says the Lord, when I will establish a new covenant with the house of Israel and with the house of Judah; not like the covenant that I made with their fathers on the day when I took them by the hand to lead them out of the land of Egypt'." [56] And a little further on, "In speaking of a new covenant He treats the old as obsolete. And what is becoming obsolete and growing old is ready to vanish away . . . for a tent was prepared, the outer one in which were the lampstand and the table and the bread of the Presence; it is called the Holy Place. Behind the second curtain stood a tent called the

---

[55] Ex. 25:40.   [56] Heb. 8:4-9.

Holy of Holies, having the golden altar of incense and the ark of the covenant covered on all sides with gold, which contained a golden urn holding the manna and Aaron's rod that budded, and the tables of the covenant; above it were the cherubim of glory overshadowing the mercy seat."[57] And again, "For Christ has entered, not into a sanctuary made with hands, a copy of the true one, but into heaven itself." [58] And after this, ". . . the law has but a shadow of the good things to come instead of the true form of these realities." [59]

23. You see that the law and everything it commanded and all our own practices are meant to sanctify the work of our hands, leading us through matter to the invisible God. Now the law and its ordinances were a shadow of the image that was to come, that is, our true worship, which itself is the image of the good things yet to happen. These good things are the heavenly Jerusalem not fashioned with hands, or built of corruptible matter, as the same divine apostle says so well, " . . . here we have no lasting city, but we seek the city which is to come," [60] which is the Jerusalem on high, "whose builder and maker is God." [61] Every observance of the law, and our service, has been instituted that we may obtain this joy. To God be glory unto ages of ages. Amen.

[57] Heb. 8:13; 9:2-5.
[58] Heb. 9:24.
[59] Heb. 10:1.

[60] Heb. 13:14.
[61] Heb. 11-10.

ANCIENT DOCUMENTATION AND TESTIMONY
OF THE HOLY FATHERS
CONCERNING IMAGES*

St. John Chrysostom, from his sermon concerning the single authorship of the Old and New Testaments; and on the garments of priests:

And I love this image molded in wax, of him who was full of righteousness. For I see the angel in the icon fighting the barbarian horde. I see him trampling down the ranks of barbarians, and David speaking truly: "O Lord, in Thy city Thou wilt despise their image." [62]

The same, from his sermon on the parable of the sower:

If you insult the royal robe, do you not insult him who wears it? Do you not know that if you insult the image of the emperor, you transfer the insult to the prototype? Do you not know that if you show contempt to his image, whether it is a wooden carving or a copper statue, you will be judged not for insulting lifeless matter, but for showing the emperor contempt? Dishonor shown to the emperor's image is dishonor shown to the emperor himself.

The same from his sermon on Meletius of Antioch, bishop and martyr, concerning the zeal of those assembled to hear him, which begins, "Casting his eyes everywhere on his holy flock . . ." And after this:

And performing the teaching of righteousness, he urged us always to remember this discourse and have this saint

---

* St. John reiterates in this second oration most of the references which conclude the first oration. Only those peculiar to this oration are included here.

[62] Ps. 72:20 (LXX).

on our minds, whose name they invoked against every ir-
rational passion and vain speech and this became so much
the case that everywhere — the streets, the market-place,
the fields — rang with his name. Not only do you long to
call fervently upon his great name; but also to look upon
the image of his bodily form. What you do with his name
you also accomplish with his image. For everyone rejoices
to put his image everywhere, on rings, goblets, dishes, and
on bedroom walls, so they can not only hear his holy dis-
courses, but also gaze everywhere on his bodily image,
thus gaining a double consolation to make up for his de-
parture from us.

St. Ambrose, bishop of Milan, from his epistle to all
Italians:

On the third night of my fast, my body was already
exhausted, but I did not sleep, but was caught up in ecstasy
during which a face was revealed to me, which resembled
the blessed apostle Paul, the same face which was painted
on the icon which showed him teaching so wisely . . .

St. Maximus the confessor and philosopher, from his
Acts, followed by those of the bishop Theodosius:

After these things everyone rose with tears of joy, and
bowing down low, they prayed, and everyone kissed the holy
Gospels, and the honorable cross, and the icons of our God
and Savior Jesus Christ, and of our Lady the All-Holy
Theotokos who gave birth to Him, and they touched these
things with their hands, in confirmation of what had been
said.

The holy and blessed Anastasius, Archbishop of Antioch, concerning the sabbath, written to Simeon, Bishop
of Bostra:

Just as in the emperor's absence we bow down to his
image instead of himself, so also when he remains present
it would be strange to ignore the prototype and bow before
the image. This is not to say that the image we ignore be-
cause the prototype is present can be dishonored. Just as

someone who insults the emperor's image is punished as if he had insulted the emperor himself, even though the image is composed merely of wood and paint joined together, so also one who insults someone's image intends the insult for the original.

THIRD APOLOGY OF SAINT JOHN OF DAMASCUS AGAINST THOSE WHO ATTACK THE DIVINE IMAGES*

10. . . . I have often seen lovers gazing at the garments of their beloved, embracing the garments with their eyes and their lips as if the garment were the beloved one. We must give every man his due, as the holy apostle Paul says: "honor to whom honor is due, whether it be to the emperor as supreme, or to governors sent by him,"[1] to each one, according to the measure of his dignity.

11. Where can you find in the Old Testament or in the Gospels explicit use of such terms as "Trinity" or "consubstantial" or "one nature of the Godhead," or "three persons," or anything about Christ being "one person with two natures?" But nevertheless, the meanings of all these things are found, expressed in other phrases which the Scriptures do contain, and the fathers have interpreted them for us. We accept them, and anathematize those who will not. I have proven to you that under the old covenant God commanded images to be made: first the tabernacle, and then everything in it. And in the Gospels the Lord Himself answered those who questioned and tested Him saying, "Is it lawful to pay taxes to Caesar?" He said to them, "Show me the money for the tax," and they brought Him a coin.

---

* In this third oration St. John repeats entire passages from his first and second orations. In general these passages are not included in this text of the third oration. The most extensive repetition involves the first nine paragraphs (and most of the tenth) of the present oration.

[1] Rom. 13:7.

And Jesus said to them, "Whose likeness and inscription is this?" They said, "Caesar's." Then He said to them, "Render therefore to Caesar the things that are Caesar's, and to God the things that are God's." [2] Since the coin bears Caesar's likeness, it is united to Caesar's person and you must give it back to him. Likewise the icon of Christ is part of Him, and you must give it what is due.

12. The Lord called His disciples blessed, for He said, "Blessed are your eyes, for they see, and your ears, for they hear. Truly, I say to you, many prophets and kings longed to see what you see, and did not see it, and to hear what you hear, and did not hear it." [3] The apostles saw Christ in the flesh; they witnessed His sufferings and His miracles, and heard His words. We too desire to see, and to hear, and so be filled with gladness. They saw Him face to face, since He was physically present. Since He is no longer physically present, we hear His words read from books and by hearing our souls are sanctified and filled with blessing, and so we worship, honoring the books from which we hear His words. So also, through the painting of images, we are able to contemplate the likeness of His bodily form, His miracles, and His passion, and thus are sanctified, blessed, and filled with joy. Reverently we honor and worship His bodily form, and by contemplating His bodily form, we form a notion, as far as is possible for us, of the glory of His divinity. Since we are fashioned of both soul and body, and our souls are not naked spirits, but are covered, as it were, with a fleshly veil, it is impossible for us to think without using physical images. Just as we physically listen to perceptible words in order to understand spiritual things, so also by using bodily sight we reach spiritual contemplation. For this reason Christ assumed both soul and body, since man is fashioned from both. Likewise baptism is both

---

[2] Mt. 22:17-21.   [3] Mt. 13:16-17.

of water and of Spirit. It is the same with communion, prayer, psalmody, candles, or incense; they all have a double significance, physical and spiritual.

13.   The devil has avoided all these things, saving his storm for icons alone. His great jealousy of icons may be learned by what the holy Sophronius, the patriarch of Jerusalem, records in his *Spiritual Garden.** You see that those who prevent the veneration of images are the imitators and instruments of the devil, for instead of further tempting the old man, the demon of lust attempted to deprive our Lady's icon of honor, since he knew which would be the greater evil.

14.   Since we are speaking of images and their veneration, let us bring forward and examine thoroughly every aspect concerning them. Let us consider these questions: 1) What is an image? 2) Why are images made? 3) How many kinds of images are there? 4) What may be depicted by an image, and what may not? 5) Who first made images?

15.   Concerning worship, let us examine the following: 1) What is worship? 2) How many kinds of worship are there? 3) How many things in Scripture can we discover that were worshipped? 4) All worship is for the sake of God, who is by nature worshipful. 5) That any honor given to an image is transferred to its prototype.

First point — What is an image?

16.   An image is a likeness, or a model, or a figure of something, showing in itself what it depicts. An image is

---

* This story is recounted near the conclusion of the first apology.

not always like its prototype in every way. For the image
is one thing, and the thing depicted is another; one can
always notice differences between them, since one is not
the other, and vice versa. I offer the following example:
An image of a man, even if it is a likeness of his bodily
form, cannot contain his mental powers. It has no life;
it cannot think, or speak, or hear, or move. A son is the
natural image of his father, yet is different from him, for
he is a son, and not a father.

Second Point — Why are images made?

17. All images reveal and make perceptible those
things which are hidden. For example, man does not have
immediate knowledge of invisible things, since the soul is
veiled by the body. Nor can man have immediate knowledge of things which are distant from each other or separated by place, because he himself is circumscribed by place
and time. Therefore the image was devised that he might
advance in knowledge, and that secret things might be
revealed and made perceptible. Therefore, images are a
source of profit, help, and salvation for all, since they make
things so obviously manifest, enabling us to perceive hidden
things. Thus, we are encouraged to desire and imitate what
is good and to shun and hate what is evil.

Third Point — How many kinds of images are there?

18. There are different kinds of images. First there is
the natural image. In every case it is necessary for a natural
image to come first, and only later those images which are
made by words or artistic representation. First we have a
human being; only then can we have words or pictures. The
Son of the Father is the first natural and precisely similar

image of the invisible God, for He reveals the Father in His own person. "No one has ever seen God," [4] and again, ". . . not that any one has seen the Father." [5] The apostle says that the Son is the image of the Father: "He is the image of the invisible God," [6] and to the Hebrews he says, ". . . who, being the brightness of His glory and the image of His substance." [7] In St. John's Gospel we see that He does manifest the Father in Himself, for when Philip says to Him, "Lord, show us the Father and it is enough for us," Jesus said to him, "Have I been so long a time with you, and you have not known Me? Philip, he who sees Me sees also the Father." [8] The Son is the natural image of the Father, precisely similar to the Father in every way, except that He is begotten by the Father, who is not begotten. For the Father begets, but Himself is unbegotten, while the Son is begotten, and is not the Father, and the Holy Spirit is the image of the Son (τὸ Πνεῦμα τὸ ἅγιον, εἰκὼν τοῦ Υἱοῦ) for no one can say "Jesus is Lord," except by the Holy Spirit. [9] Through the Holy Spirit we know Christ, who is God and the Son of God, and in the Son we see the Father. The Word is the messenger who makes the divine nature perceptible to us, and the Spirit is the interpreter of the Word. The Holy Spirit is the precisely similar image of the Son, differing only in His manner of procession, for the Son is begotten; He does not proceed. And the son of any father is his natural image. Therefore the first kind of image is the natural image.

19. The second kind of image is God's foreknowledge of things which have yet to happen, His changeless purpose from before all ages. The divine nature is immutable, and His purpose is without beginning. His plans are made before all ages, and they come to pass at the time which has

---

[4] Jn. 1:18. [6] Col. 1:15. [8] Jn. 14:8-9.
[5] Jn. 6:46. [7] Heb. 1:3. [9] I Cor. 12:3.

been predetermined for them by Him. Images and figures of things He has yet to do, and the purpose of each of them, were called predeterminations by holy Dionysius. In God's providence, those things predetermined by Him were characterized, depicted, and unalterably fixed before they even came to pass.

20.   The third kind of image is made by God as an imitation of Himself: namely, man. How can what is created share the nature of Him who is uncreated, except by imitation? Just as the Father, and the Son who is the Word, and the Holy Spirit, are one God, so also mind and spirit constitute one man, according to God's dominion and authority. For God says, "Let us make man according to our own image and likeness," and immediately He adds, "and let him have dominion over the fish of the sea, and over the birds of the air, and over all the earth." [10]

21.   The fourth kind of image consists of the shadows and forms and types of invisible and bodiless things which are described by the Scriptures in physical terms. These give us a faint apprehension of God and the angels where otherwise we would have none, because it is impossible for us to think immaterial things unless we can envision analogous shapes, as the great and holy Dionysius the Areopagite has said. Anyone would say that our inability immediately to direct our thoughts to contemplation of higher things makes it necessary that familiar every-day media be utilized to give suitable form to what is formless, and make visible what cannot be depicted, so that we are able to construct understandable analogies. If, therefore, the Word of God, in providing for our every need, always presents to us what is intangible by clothing it with form, does it not accomplish this by making an image using what is common to nature

---

[10] Gen. 1:26.

and so bringing within our reach that for which we long but are unable to see?[11] The eloquent Gregory says that the mind which is determined to ignore corporeal things will find itself weakened and frustrated. Since the creation of the world the invisible things of God are clearly seen by means of images. We see images in the creation which, although they are only dim lights, still remind us of God. For instance, when we speak of the holy and eternal Trinity, we use the images of the sun, light, and burning rays; or a running fountain; or an overflowing river; or the mind, speech, and spirit within us; or a rose tree, a flower, and a sweet fragrance.[12]

22. The fifth kind of image is said to prefigure what is yet to happen, such as the burning bush or the fleece wet with dew, which are foreshadowings of the Virgin Theotokos, as the rod of Aaron and the jar of manna. The brazen serpent typifies the cross and Him who healed the evil bite of the serpent by hanging on it. Baptismal grace is signified by the cloud and the waters of the sea.

23. The sixth kind of image is made for the remembrance of past events, such as miracles or good deeds, in order that glory, honor and eternal memory may be given to those who have struggled valiantly. They assist the increase of virtue, that evil men might be put to shame and overthrown, and they benefit generations to come, that by gazing upon such images we may be encouraged to flee evil and desire good. These images are of two kinds: either they are words written in books, in which case the written word is the image, as when God had the law engraved on tablets [13] and desired the lives and deeds of holy men to be recorded,[14]

---

[11] Cf. *On the Ecclesiastical Hierarchies*, Ch. 1.

[12] *Theological Orations*, 2.

[13] Deut. 5:22.   [14] Ex. 17:14.

or else they are material images, such as the jar of manna, or Aaron's staff, which were to be kept in the ark as an everlasting memorial,[15] or the two onyx stones engraved with the names of the tribes which were set on the shoulder-pieces of the ephod,[16] or the twelve stones which he commanded to be taken from the Jordan for a second memorial[17] (such a mystery, truly the greatest ever to befall the faithful people!) of the carrying of the ark and the parting of the waters. Therefore we now set up images in remembrance of valiant men, that we may zealously desire to follow their example. Either remove these images altogether, and reject the authority of Him who commanded them to be made, or else accept them in the manner and with the esteem which they deserve.

Fourth Point — What may be depicted by an image, and what may not, and how images are to be made?

24. Physical things which have shape, bodies which are circumscribed, and have color, are suitable subjects for image-making. Nevertheless, even if nothing physical or fleshly may be attributed to an angel, or a soul, or a demon, it is still possible to depict and circumscribe them according to their nature. For they are intellectual beings, and are believed to be invisibly present and to operate spiritually. It is possible to make bodily representations of them just as Moses depicted the cherubim. Those who were worthy saw these images, and beheld a bodiless and intellectual sight made manifest through physical means. The divine nature alone can never be circumscribed and is always without form, without shape, and can never be understood. If Holy Scripture clothes God with forms which appear to be

---

[15] Ex. 16:33-34; Num. 17:10.
[16] Ex. 28:11-12.   [17] Jos. 4:20ff.

physical, or even visible shape, these forms are still immaterial in an important sense, because they were not seen by everyone, nor could they be perceived with the unaided bodily eye, but they were seen through the spiritual sight of prophets or others to whom they were revealed. In a word, it may be said that we may make images of every form we see, and our apprehension of these forms is a kind of sight. If we sometimes understand forms by using our minds, but other times from what we see, then it is through these two ways that we are brought to understanding. It is the same with the other senses: after we have smelled or tasted, or touched, we combine our experience with reason, and thus come to knowledge.

25. We know that it is impossible to look upon God, or a spirit, or a demon, as they are by nature. We would be able to see them, however, if they appeared in forms alien to their nature. Therefore God in His providence has clothed in forms and shapes things which are bodiless and without form, in order to lead us to more particular knowledge, lest we should be totally ignorant of God and of bodiless creatures. Only God by nature is utterly without a body, but an angel, or a soul, or a demon, when compared to God (who alone cannot be compared to anything) does have a body, but when these are compared to material bodies, they are bodiless. God wills that we should not be totally ignorant of bodiless creatures, and so He clothed them with forms and shapes, and used images comprehensible to our nature, material forms which could be seen by the spiritual vision of the mind. From these we make images and representations, for how else could the cherubim be shown as having form? But Scripture also has forms and images of God Himself.

Fifth Point — Who first made images?

26.   In the beginning He who is God begot His only
Son, His Word, the living image of Himself, the natural and
precisely similar likeness of His eternity. And He made man
after His own image and likeness.[18] And Adam saw God,
and heard the sound of His feet as He walked in Paradise
in the cool of the evening, and hid himself.[19] Jacob saw
and struggled with God, for it is evident that God appeared
to him as a man.[20] Moses saw, as it were, the back of a
man; [21] Isaiah saw Him as a man sitting upon a throne.[22]
Daniel saw the likeness of a man, and one like a son of man
coming before the Ancient of Days.[23] No one saw the divine
nature, but the image and figure of what was yet to come.
For the invisible Son and Word of God was to become truly
man, that He might be united to our nature, and be seen on
earth. All who saw this image or figure of what was to come
worshipped it, as Paul the apostle says in the Epistle to
the Hebrews: "These all died in faith, not having received
what was promised, but having seen it and greeted it from
afar." [24] Shall I not make an image of Him who was seen
in the nature of flesh for me? Shall I not worship and honor
Him, through the honor and veneration of His image?
Abraham did not see the divine nature, for no man has
ever yet seen God, but he saw an image of God, and fell
down and worshipped.[25] Joshua the son of Nun did not see
the angel [26] as he is by nature, but an image, for an angel
by nature is not visible to bodily eyes, yet he fell down and
worshipped, and Daniel did likewise. Yet an angel is a
creature, a servant and minister of God, but not God. And
they fell down in worship before the angels, not as God,
but as God's ministering spirits. Shall I not make images

---

[18] Gen. 1:26.   [21] Ex. 33:24ff.   [24] Heb. 11:13.
[19] Cf. Gen. 3:8.   [22] Is. 6:1.   [25] Gen. 18:2.
[20] Gen. 32:24ff.   [23] Dan. 7:9, 13.   [26] Jos. 5:14.

of friends? Shall I not honor them, not as gods, but as the images of God's friends? Neither Joshua nor Daniel worshipped the angels they saw as gods. Neither do I worship an image as God, but through the images of Christ and of the holy Theotokos, and of the saints, I bring worship and honor to God, because of the reverence with which I honor His friends. God did not unite Himself with angelic nature, but with human nature. God did not become an angel; He became a man by nature and in truth. For surely it is not with angels that He is concerned, but with the seed of Abraham.[27] The person of the Son of God did not assume angelic nature, but human nature. Angels do not share in this; they do not become partakers of the divine nature. But by the operation of grace, men do share in and become partakers of the divine nature, as many of them as receive the holy Body of Christ and drink His Blood, since His person is united with the Godhead, and the two natures of Christ's Body which we eat are inseparably joined in His person. We partake of both natures, of His Body physically, and of His divinity spiritually, or rather, of each in both. We do not become the same person as He is, for we also first exist as individual persons; only then can we be united by the commingling of His Body and Blood. Therefore, we are greater than the angels, provided that we guard this perfect union by faithfully observing the commandments. For our humble nature is far inferior to the angels, because of death, and the heaviness of the body, but because by God's good will it has been united to Him, human nature has become superior to the angels. The angels stand in fear and trembling before our own nature, for He has raised us up with Him and made us sit with Him in the heavenly places in Christ Jesus,[28] and they will stand by in fear at the judgement. Nowhere does Scripture say that they will sit together with us, or become partakers of the divine nature. Are they

---

[27] Heb. 2:16.   [28] Eph. 2:6.

not all ministering spirits sent forth to serve, for the sake of those who are to obtain salvation?[29] It is not their place to reign or be glorified together with those who shall sit at the Father's table; the saints, on the other hand, are sons of God, sons of the Kingdom, heirs of God, and fellow heirs of Christ,[30] for they are servants by nature, friends by election, and sons and fellow-heirs by divine grace, as the Lord said to the Father.[31]

Now that we have spoken of images, let us speak of worship. In the first place, let us determine what it is.

ON WORSHIP. What is Worship?

27.   Worship is a sign of submission. Submission implies abasement and humiliation. There are many different kinds of worship.

On the kinds of worship

28.   The first kind of absolute worship is adoration, which we give to God alone. Only He by nature deserves to be worshipped. This worship is given in several ways. The first is the worship given by servants. All created things worship Him, as servants worship their Master, for "all things are Thy servants." [32] The worship of some is voluntary; of others it is involuntary. The righteous worship willingly and with knowledge, whereas others, such as the demons, also worship with knowledge, but not willingly or voluntarily. Still others do not know who God is, but even in their ignorance give Him involuntary worship.

29.   The second kind of absolute worship is the awe and

---

[29] Heb. 1:14.   [30] Rom. 8:17.   [31] Cf. Jn. 17.   [32] Ps. 119:91.

yearning we have for God because of the glory which is His by nature. He alone is worthy to be glorified, but no one can of himself glorify Him, because He Himself is the source of all glory, all goodness, unapproachable light, incomparable sweetness, boundless perfection, an abyss of goodness, inscrutable wisdom, infinite power, who alone is worthy in Himself to be admired, worshipped, glorified and desired.

30. The third kind of absolute worship is thanksgiving for all the good things He has created for us. All things owe a debt of thanks to God, and must offer Him ceaseless worship, because all things have their existence from Him, and in Him all things hold together.[33] He gives lavishly of His gifts to all, without being asked; He desires all men to be saved [34] and to partake of His goodness. He is long-suffering with us sinners, for He makes His sun rise on the evil and on the good, and sends rain on the just and on the unjust.[35] He is the Son of God, yet He became one of us for our sake, and made us participants of His divine nature, so that "we shall be like Him," [36] as John the Theologian says in his catholic epistle.

31. The fourth kind of absolute worship is inspired by our needs and hopes for His blessing. Since we realize that without His help we possess no goodness and are able to do nothing, we worship Him, beseeching Him to listen to each one of our needs and desires, that we may be delivered from evil and attain to goodness.

32. The fifth kind of absolute worship is repentance and confession. As sinners we worship and prostrate ourselves before God, begging Him to forgive our sins, as is fitting for servants to do. This happens in three ways. A

[33] Cf. Col. 1:16-17. [35] Mt. 5:45.
[34] I Tim. 2:4. [36] I Jn. 3:2.

man may be sorry because he loves God, or because he has
failed to obtain God's blessings, or because he fears chastise-
ment. The first is inspired by gratitude and desire for God,
and is the disposition of a son; the second is the disposition
of a tenant farmer, and the third is the disposition of a slave.

How many things in Scripture can we find that were
worshipped in a relative sense? What are the different ways
we offer this relative worship to created things?

33.   First of all, those places where God, who alone is
holy, has rested. He rests in holy places: that is, the Theotokos, and all the saints. These are they who have become
likenesses of God as far as is possible, since they have chosen
to cooperate with divine election. Therefore God dwells in
them. They are truly called gods, not by nature, but by
adoption, just as red-hot iron is called fiery, not by its
nature, but because it participates in the action of the fire.
He says "You shall be holy, for I the Lord your God am
holy." [37] First, then, is the election to holiness. Then, once
the right choice has been made, God helps those who make
it to increase in goodness, for He says, "I will make my
abode among you." [38] We are God's temple and the Spirit
of God dwells in us.[39] "He gave them authority over unclean spirits, to cast them out, and to heal every disease and
infirmity," [40] and, "he who believes in Me will also do the
works that I do: and greater works than these will he do." [41]
And again, " 'As I live' says the Lord, 'those who honor Me,
I will honor'," [42] and, "provided we suffer with Him in order
that we may also be glorified with Him," [43] and, "God has
taken His place in the divine council; in the midst of the gods
He holds judgement." [44] Therefore, since they are truly gods,
not by nature, but because they partake of the divine nature,

[37] Lev. 19:2.   [40] Mt. 10:1.   [43] Rom. 8:17.
[38] Lev. 26:12.   [41] Jn. 14:12.   [44] Ps. 82:1.
[39] Cf. I Cor. 3:16.   [42] I Sam. 2:30.

they are to be venerated, not because they deserve it on their
own account, but because they bear in themselves Him who
is by nature worshipful. We do not back away and refuse
to touch red hot iron because of the nature of iron, but
because it has partaken of what is hot by nature. The saints
are to be venerated because God has glorified them, and
through Him they have become fearful to the enemy, and
are benefactors for the faithful. They are not gods and
benefactors by their own nature, but because they were
loving servants and ministers of God, they have been en-
dowed with boldness before Him. Therefore we venerate
them, because the king is given honor through the worship
given to his beloved servants. They are obedient servants
and favored friends, but they are not the King Himself.
When some one prays with faith, offering his petition in
the name of such a favored friend, the King receives it,
through the intercession of the faithful servant, because He
accepts the honor and faith which the petitioner has shown
to His servant. Thus, those who approach God through the
apostles enjoyed healing, for the shadow of the apostles,
or even handkerchiefs and aprons touched to them,[45] gushed
with cures. Those who rebelliously and perversely wished
to worship them as gods are themselves execrable, and
deserve eternal fire, but those who because of their presump-
tuous arrogance and contempt refuse to honor God's servants, will be convicted as arrogant imposters, who have
shown dishonor to God. The children who mocked and
laughed Elisha to scorn are a testimony of this, for they were
devoured by bears.[46]

34. The second kind of relative worship we give to
created things concerns those places and things by which
God has accomplished our salvation, whether before the
coming of the Lord, or since the dispensation of His in-

---

[45] Acts 5:15.   [46] II Kgs. 2:23.

carnation, such as Mount Sinai, and Nazareth, the cave and manger of Bethlehem, the holy mountain of Golgotha, the wood of the cross, the nails, the sponge, the reed, the holy and saving lance, the robe, the seamless tunic, the winding-sheet, the swaddling-clothes, the holy tomb which is the fountain of our resurrection, the stone which sealed the sepulchre, holy Mount Zion and the holy Mount of Olives, the pool of Bethsaida, the blessed garden of Gethsemane, and all other similar places. I honor and venerate all God's holy temples, and everything where God's name is found, not for their own sake, but because they are vessels of divine power. Through them and in them God was pleased to accomplish our salvation. I honor and venerate angels, and men, and all matter which partakes of divine power, for these things have assisted in my salvation, and God has worked through them. I do not honor the Jews, for they refused to partake of divine power, and had no wish for my salvation. They crucified my God, the Lord of glory; they attacked God their benefactor with envy and hatred. "O Lord, I love the beauty of Thy house," says David, "and the place where Thy glory dwells," [47] and, "Let us go to His dwelling place; let us worship at His footstool," [48] and, "... worship at His holy mountain." [49] The holy Theotokos is the living mountain of God, and the apostles are the speaking mountains of God. "The mountains skipped like rams, the hills like lambs of the flock." [50]

35.   The third kind of relative worship we give to objects dedicated to God, such as the holy Gospel and other books, for they have been written for our instruction, upon whom the end of the ages has come.[51] Obviously, patens, chalices, censers, candlesticks, and altars should all receive respect. Remember how Belshazzar made his people serve

---

[47] Ps. 26:8.   [49] Ps. 99:9.   [51] I Cor. 10:11.
[48] Ps. 132:7.   [50] Ps. 114:4.

wine in the sacred vessels, and how God brought his kingdom to an end.[52]

36. The fourth kind of relative worship is given to those images which were seen by the prophets (for they saw God in the images of their visions). These images were of future things, such as Aaron's rod, which prefigured the mystery of the Virgin, or the jar of manna, or the altar. Jacob bowed in homage over the point of Joseph's staff.[53] Joseph was a figure of the Savior. Images of past events assure that they will be remembered. The tabernacle was an image common to all the world. "And see," God said to Moses, "that you make everything according to the pattern which was shown you on the mountain."[54] This included the golden cherubim of hammered work, and the cherubim woven on the veil of the holy of holies. Thus, we venerate the honorable figure of the cross, or the likeness of the physical features of our God, or of her who gave birth to Him in the flesh, and everyone who is part of Him.

37. The fifth kind of relative worship is our veneration of each other, since we are God's inheritance, and were made according to His image, and so we are subject to each other,[55] thus fulfilling the law of love.

38. The sixth kind of relative worship is given to those who have been given authority to rule over us. The apostle says, "pay all of them their due, . . . honor to whom honor is due." [56] So Jacob bowed down before Esau his elder brother, as well as Pharaoh, the ruler whom God had appointed.

---

[52] Dan. 5:2ff.   [55] Eph. 5:21.
[53] Gen. 47:31 (LXX).   [56] Rom. 13:7.
[54] Ex. 25:40.

39. The seventh kind of relative worship is given to masters by their servants, and to benefactors who grant the requests of their petitioners, as was the case when Abraham did reverence to the Hittites, when he bought the cave of Machpelah from Ephron.[57]

40. It is needless to say that fear, desire, and honor all are signs of worship, as are submission and abnegation. But no one should worship anyone as God. Worship as God only Him who is God by nature. Whatever is reckoned to be due all the rest is given for the Lord's sake.

41. You see what strength and divine power is given to him who accepts the images of the saints with faith and a pure conscience. Therefore, brethren, let us stand on the rock of faith and on the tradition of the Church, not removing the ancient landmarks which our holy fathers have set,[58] nor allowing any room for those who would decree innovations and destroy the structure of the holy catholic and apostolic Church of God. If all those who would make decrees are allowed such license, in a short time the entire structure of the Church would come to an end. No, brother, no, Christ-loving children of the Church, do not expose your mother to shame, do not rend her in pieces. Welcome her authority which I have defended. Learn what God says concerning her: "You are all fair, my love; there is no stain in you."[59] Let us worship and adore our Creator and fashioner of all; for He alone by nature is to be worshipped as God. Let us honor the holy Theotokos, not as God, but as the Mother of God according to the flesh. Let us also venerate the saints, for they are God's chosen friends, and possess boldness before Him. If men honor emperors, who are often corrupt and impious sinners, as well as those appointed by them to rule over provinces, who often are

---

[57] Gen. 23:7, 12.   [58] Prov. 22:28.   [59] Cant. 4:7.

greedy and violent men, in obedience to the words of the
divine apostle, "Be submissive to rulers and authorities," [60]
and, "Pay all of them their dues, honor to whom honor
is due; respect to whom respect is due," [61] and "Render
therefore to Ceasar the things that are Caesar's, and to God
the things that are God's," [62] how much more ought we to
worship the King of Kings? He alone is Master by nature;
His servants and friends have triumphed over their passions
and have been appointed rulers over all the earth. "You
will make them princes in all the earth," [63] says David. They
have received power over all demons and diseases,[64] and
they reign with Christ over an incorruptible and eternal
kingdom. Their shadow alone expels demons and diseases.[65]
Would not a shadow be reckoned weaker and less honorable than an icon? An icon is a more distinct portrayal of
the prototype. Brothers, the Christian is a man of faith.
He who walks by faith gains everything. But he who doubts
is like a wave of the sea that is driven and tossed by the
wind, and will not receive anything from the Lord.[66] All
the saints were pleasing to God because of their faith.
Let us receive the tradition of the Church in simplicity of
heart, without vain questioning, since God created man to
be straightforward, but he has entangled himself with an
infinity of questions.[67] Let us not allow ourselves to learn
a new faith, in opposition to the tradition of the fathers.
The divine apostle says: "If anyone is preaching to you a
gospel contrary to that which you received, let him be
anathema." [68] We venerate images; it is not veneration
offered to matter, but to those who are portrayed through
matter in the images. Any honor given to an image is transferred to its prototype, as St. Basil says.

---

[60] Tit. 3:1.   [63] Ps. 45:16.   [66] Jas. 1:6-8.
[61] Rom. 13:7.   [64] Cf. Lk. 9:1.   [67] Cf. Eccl. 7:30.
[62] Mt. 22:21.   [65] Acts 5:16.   [68] Gal. 1:9.

42. May Christ fill you, His priestly flock, the Christian people, the holy nation, the body of the Church, with the joy of His resurrection, and make us worthy to follow in the footsteps of the saints, the shepherds and teachers of the Church, leading us to enjoy His glory in the radiance of the saints. May you attain His love and glorify Him forever, with the unoriginate Father, to whom be glory unto ages of ages. Amen.

Having spoken about the difference between idols and icons, and having taught what an icon is, it is now time to add further testimony, as has been promised to you.

ANCIENT DOCUMENTATION AND TESTIMONY OF THE HOLY FATHERS CONCERNING IMAGES*

St. Dionysius, bishop of Athens, from his letter to St. John the apostle and theologian:

Truly, sensory images make invisible things visible.

St. Basil, from his sermon on the Forty Holy Martyrs:

The brave deeds accomplished in time of war are celebrated by both orators and artists. Orators remember them with decorous words; artists with paintbrush and canvas, and both inspire everyone with valor. That which words are to the ear, silent pictures reveal for imitation.

The same, from the *Thirty Chapters to Amphilochius on the Holy Spirit*, from Chapter 18.**

The image of the emperor is also called the emperor, yet there are not two emperors. Power is not divided, nor is glory separated. Just as He who rules us is one power, so the homage He receives from us is one, not multiple, for the honor given to the image is transferred to the prototype. Therefore, the One whom the image materially represents is the Son by nature.

Commentary: Just as, "He who does not honor the Son does not honor the Father who sent Him," [69] so he who refuses to honor the image also refuses honor to him who is portrayed. But it may be that someone will say, "It is necessary to honor the icon of Christ, but not those

---

* As the introduction explains, only a selection of St. John's very extensive bibliography is included here.

** This reference is also found following the first apology, in a longer form and with a different commentary.

[69] Jn. 5:23.

of the saints." What madness! Listen to what the Lord says
to His disciples, "He who receives you receives me." [70] He
who does not honor the saints does not honor Christ either.

Theodoret, Bishop of Cyrus, from *The History of Those
Who Love God*, found in the life of St. Simeon the Stylite:

*It is superfluous to speak of Italy, for they say that this
man was so well-known in the great city of Rome that
on the gates of all the workshops, small icons of him were
put up to obtain protection and security for those who
erected them!*

St. Basil the Great, from his *Commentary on Isaiah:*

*When he saw that man was made in the image and like-
ness of God, the devil realized that it was useless for him
to fight against God, so instead he entangled God's image
in evil. In the same way, an angry man might throw stones
at the emperor's image, since he cannot throw them at the
emperor, and so must be content with striking the wood
which bears his likeness.*

Commentary: Thus it is obvious that everyone who
honors an image also honors its prototype.

And again, from the same commentary:

*Just as he who shows comtempt to the royal image is
judged to have insulted the emperor himself, so he who
shows contempt to man created after God's image will
also be convicted of sin.*

St. Athanasius, from his hundred chapters written to
Antiochus the Prefect in the form of questions and answers,
from Chapter 38:

*Answer: We the faithful do not worship images as gods,
as did the heathen Greeks — God forbid! — but our only
purpose and desire is to see in the image a reflection of the
facial form of the beloved. Therefore if the image should
be obliterated, we would throw it into the fire as so much
scrap lumber. Just as when Jacob was about to die, he*

---

[70] Mt. 10:40.

bowed down before the point of Joseph's staff, not honoring the staff but its owner, so also the faithful do not embrace images for their own sake, but kiss them as we often embrace our children or our parents, to show the affection in our hearts. So also the Jew, when he venerated the tables of the law, or the two cherubim, hammered from gold, did not honor stone or gold for its own sake, but the Lord who had ordered them to be made.

St. John Chrysostom, on the Third Psalm, concerning David and Absalom:

Kings erect statues to celebrate the triumphs of their victorious generals; rulers build monuments to victorious charioteers and athletes, decorating them with epitaphs and wreaths, thus using material things to proclaim their victories. Again, others praise their victories in books and scrolls, wishing to show that their ability to write eloquent praises is an even greater feat than the deeds of those praised. So orators, painters, and sculptors, people, rulers, cities, and countries marvel at such victories. But no one ever made images of deserters or cowards.

St. Cyril of Alexandria, from his address to the emperor Theodosius:

Images are representations of their archetypes and therefore are similar to them. This relationship is necessary; it could never be otherwise.

The same, from his *Treasures:*

Images are always related to the archetypes of which they are the likenesses.

The same, from his work, "On How the Mystery of Christ was Prefigured Through All the Writtings of Moses." From Chapter 6, concerning Abraham and Melchizedek:

It seems fitting to me that images should be painted which resemble their archetypes.

St. Gregory of Nazianzus, from his second sermon concerning the Son:

For the nature of the image is to be an artistic representation of its archetype.

St. John Chrysostom, from his third sermon on the Epistle to the Colossians:

If an image of something invisible became invisible as well, it would cease to be an image. For an image, inasmuch as it is an image, ought to be treated by us in the same fashion as the likeness it represents.

The same, from his commentary on the Epistle to the Hebrews, Chapter 17:

The image has the figure of the man, but not the power, but since the figure exists equally in both the original and the image, they have this much in common.

Eusebius of Pamphylia, from the fifth book of his exposition on the Gospels, where he says "God appeared to Abraham at the oak of Mamre": [71]

Even now the inhabitants of those regions near where Abraham worshipped those who appeared to him honor it as a holy place. Indeed, the oak tree is still to be seen there, and there is a picture of those whom Abraham entertained reclining at table, one shown on each side and the most august and honorable guest in the middle. Through him is signified to us our Lord and Savior, whom simple men honor and whose divine words they believe. Hidden in human appearance and form, he showed himself to Abraham the Godloving forefather, and gave him knowledge of the Father. Thus through Abraham He planted the seed of righteousness in men.

Eusebius, from Chapter 18 of the book of his *Church History* concerning the woman of Caesarea Philippi who had the issue of blood:

. . . Since I have mentioned this city, I do not think it proper to omit an account which deserves to be remembered

---

[71] Gen. 18:1.

by posterity. For they say that the woman with an issue of blood, who, as we learn in the holy Gospel, received from our Savior deliverance from her affliction, came from that place, and that her house may be seen in the city, and that a remarkable memorial of the Savior's kindness to her remains there. By the gates of her house there stands upon an elevated stone a bronze image of a woman kneeling with outstretched hands, as if she were praying. Opposite this there is another upright image of a man, made of the same material, clothed decently in a double cloak and extending his hand toward the woman. At his feet, beside the statue itself, is a certain strange plant, which climbs up to the hem of the bronze cloak, and is a remedy for all kinds of diseases. They say that this statue is an image of the Lord Jesus. It has remained to our day, so that we ourselves also saw it when we were staying in the city. Nor is it strange that those Gentiles who were blessed by our Savior of old should do such things, since we have also learned that the likenesses of His apostles Peter and Paul, and of Christ Himself, are preserved in paintings, for it is likely that the ancients were accustomed, according to the habits of the Gentiles, to pay this kind of honor indiscriminately to those regarded by them as saviors.

From the same history, the ninth chapter of the ninth book, concerning the emperor Constantine:

. . . but he, as one possessed of inborn piety toward God, did not exult in the shouts, nor was he elated by the praises, but realizing that his help was given by God, he immediately commanded that a trophy of the Savior's passion be put in the hand of his own statue. And when he had placed this statue bearing the saving sign of the cross in its right hand, in the most public place of Rome, he commanded that the following inscription should be engraved on it in the Latin tongue: "By this saving sign, the true proof of bravery, I have saved and freed your city from the tyrant's yoke; and moreover, having set at liberty the senate and the Roman

people, I have restored them to their ancient distinction and splendor.

Stephen of Bostra, *Against the Jews*, chapter 4.

We make images of the saints to remember such people as Abraham, Isaac, Jacob, Moses, Elijah, Zechariah, the rest of the prophets and holy martyrs, who gave their lives to God. Everyone who looks at these images remembers these saints, and they glorify the One who glorified them.

The same:

As far as images are concerned, let us be reassured that every work begun in God's name is good and holy. Concerning idols and images dedicated to them however, away with them! They are all absurd and evil, both the idols, and those who make them; for an image of a holy prophet is one thing; a statue or carving of Cronus or Aphrodite, the sun or the moon, is another. Man is venerable only because he is made in God's image; but the serpent, since it is the image of the devil, is unclean and worthless. If you reject the handiwork of men, tell me, O Jew, what is there left on earth to venerate which is not human handiwork? Was not the ark of the covenant made with hands, and the altar, and the mercy seat, and the cherubim, and the golden jar which held the manna, and the table, and the inner sanctuary, and everything that God ordered to be placed in the holy of holies? Were not the cherubim images of angels which were fashioned by human hands? How do you reply? Will you call them idols? What will you say to Moses and to Israel, who bowed down before them? Worship is the outward sign by which honor is given. We sinners worship God, and we glorify Him with divine adoration and fitting praise. We tremble before Him, our Creator and benefactor. But we venerate the angels and servants of God in order to give Him honor, for they are His creatures and servants. An image is a representation and a likeness of him who is painted. Thus, both by painting and engraving we keep the Lord's passion in everlasting remembrance as well as the holy prophets who have been described in both the law and the Gospels.

St. Gregory of Nazianzus, from his oration against Julian the Apostate:

The images venerated in public places still bear scars of that plague.

St. Leontius, bishop of Neapolis on the island of Cyprus, from his fifth book against the Jews:

We shall now eagerly complete the remainder of our apology concerning the making of images, in order that the deceitful mouths of the lawless may be shut once and for all. For this tradition begins in the law, not with us. Consider what God said to Moses, commanding him to have the images of two cherubim hammered from gold, to overshadow the mercy-seat. And again, God showed a vision of the temple to Ezechiel, and from floor to ceiling the walls were covered with cherubim having the faces of lions and men, and pictures of palm trees. Truly this command is awesome: God, who commands Israel to make no image, or carving, or likeness of anything in heaven or on earth, Himself commands Moses to make graven images of cherubim which are living creatures. He shows a vision of the temple to Ezechiel, and it is full of the images and carved likenesses of lions, men and palm trees. Solomon knew the law, and yet he made images, filling the temple with metal figures of oxen, and palm trees, and men, but God did not reproach him for this. Now, if you wish to condemn me on this subject, you are condemning God, who ordered these things to be made, that they might be reminders for us of Himself.

The same, from the fifth book:

Again, the unbelievers mock us because we honor the cross, and they infer that because we venerate the holy images, we are idolaters and worshippers of wooden gods. If I worship wooden gods, as you say, O unbeliever, that means I worship many gods. Now if this is true, then I should swear by all of them and say "By the gods!" just as you did when you saw one calf, crying, "These are your gods, O Israel!" You have never heard Christian mouths use this expression; but it is the adulterous and faithless synagogue, which is always ready to cast aspersions on the all-wise Church of Christ.

The same:

We do not worship as gods the figures and images of the saints. For if it is the wood of the image that we worship as God, then we would worship all other wood as well, and we would not throw the image into the fire when the picture fades, as we often do. And again, as long as wood is fastened together in the form of a cross, I venerate it because it is a likeness of the wood on which Christ was crucified. If it should fall to pieces, I throw the pieces into the fire. When a man receives a sealed order from the emperor, he kisses the seal. He does not honor clay, paper, or wax for their own sake, but he gives honor and veneration to the emperor. Likewise when Christian people venerate the form of the cross, they are not worshipping the nature of wood, but they see that it is marked with the imprint of the hands of Him who was nailed upon it, and so they embrace and honor it.

The same:

For this reason I depict Christ and His suffering in churches, in homes, market-places, and storehouses, in images on cloths and vestments, and in every place, so that the remembrance of them is always before my eyes, and never is neglected, as you have always disregarded the Lord your God. When you honor the scrolls of the law, you do not worship parchment and ink, but the word of God which they contain. When I honor the image of Christ, I am not worshipping wood and paint. God forbid! But when I venerate an inanimate image of Christ, it seems that I touch and worship Christ Himself. When Jacob received Joseph's

coat of many colors from his brothers who had sold him[72]
*he caressed it and wept as he gazed upon it. He was not
weeping because of the coat, but it seemed to him that by
embracing the coat he embraced Joseph, and held him in
his arms. In the same way, when we Christians embrace
the icons of Christ or an apostle, or a martyr, with a physical
kiss, we give a spiritual kiss to Christ Himself, or His martyr.
In any event, as I have always said, one must examine the
intention of all embracings and all worship. If you accuse
me of worshipping the wood of the cross, why do you not
reproach Jacob for bowing down before the point of
Joseph's staff? It is obvious that it was not the wood he
honored by his worship, but through the wood he was
bowing before Joseph, just as we worship Christ through the
cross. Abraham bowed down before the faithless men who
sold him the cave which became a tomb, and bent his knee
to the ground, but he did not worship them as gods. Jacob
blessed Pharoah, who was an impious idolater, but he did
not bless him as God. Again, he bowed to the ground seven
times before Esau, yet did not worship him as God. See
how many embraces and how much worship I have made
evident to you, both from Scriptural evidence and natural
instinct! You will condemn none of these, yet no sooner do
you see someone venerating the icon of Christ, or his all-
holy Mother, or one of the saints, than you become angry,
and blaspheme, calling me an idolater. How can you not
blush yith shame? Every day you see me tearing down
the temples of idols all through the land, and building
churches to honor the martyrs. If I worship idols, why do
I honor the martyrs, who destroyed idols? If I glorify wood,
as you accuse me, how can I honor the saints, who threw
the wooden carvings of the demons into the fire? If it is
stones I glorify, how can I glorify the apostles, who smashed
the stone idols? If I honor the images of false gods, how*

---

[72] Gen. 37:32ff.

can I glorify, and praise, and enjoin that the feast of the three holy children in Babylon be kept, who refused to worship the golden image, because it was an idol? How hardened lawless people become, and how blind! What shamelessness is yours, O Jew; what impiety! Truly you sin against the truth. Arise, O God; plead Thy cause; judge and deliver us from a faithless people, who provoke Thee constantly.

The same:

As I have always said, if it is true that I worship wood and stone as my God, it would only be logical for me to address the wood and stone as my Creator, saying, "You are my father; you have begotten me." [73] If I venerate the images of the saints, or rather the saints themselves, and honor the struggles of the holy martyrs, how can you call these things idolatry? You fools! Idols are likenesses of false gods, and adulterers, murderers and child-killers, and those who are perverse, not of prophets or apostles. Listen while I give a succinct and credible illustration showing the difference between Christian and heathen images. The Chaldeans in Babylon used all sorts of musical instruments to worship their devilish idols; the children of Israel also brought instruments from Jerusalem: lyres, harps, and flutes, which they hung upon the willows. Some instruments had been used to give glory to God; and others were used to worship the devils, yet all the instruments were similar. So also you must discern between Christian icons and heathen idols. Understand that idols give glory to the devil and perpetuate his memory, while images glorify Christ, His apostles, His martyrs and His saints.

St. Athanasius of Alexandria, from his third book against the Arians:

Since the Son is begotten of the same essence as the Father, He can rightly speak of Himself as being equal to

---

[73] Jer. 2:27.

the Father. Therefore it is fitting that after He says, "I and the Father are one," [74] *He adds what is consequent to this: "I am in the Father and the Father in Me."* [75] *He has said the same thing before: "He who has seen Me has seen the Father."* [76] *One and the same mind express all three sayings, for to know that the Father and the Son are one is to know that the Son is in the Father and the Father in the Son. The divinity of the Son is the divinity of the Father; the Father's divinity is in the Son. He who accepts this understands that he who sees the Son sees the Father also, for the divinity of the Father is made visible in the Son. If we use the example of the emperor's image we will find this easier to understand. This image bears his form and appearance. Whatever the emperor looks like, that is how his image appears. The likeness of the emperor on the image is precisely similar to the emperor's own appearance, so that anyone who looks at the image recognizes that it is the emperor's image; also anyone who sees the emperor first and the image later, realizes at once whose image it is. Since the likenesses are interchangeable, the image might answer someone who wished to see the emperor after he had seen the image, "The emperor and I are one, for I am in him, and he is in me. That which you see in me you will also see in him, and if you should see him, you will recognize us to be the same." He who venerates the image venerates the emperor depicted on it, for the image is his form and his likeness.*

The same, to Antiochus the Prefect:

How could our adversaries reply to this? They would forbid us to venerate the images of the saints, which have been painted that we may remember those who are portrayed.

St. Ambrose, bishop of Milan, to the Emperor Gratian, concerning the incarnation of God the Word:

He was God before He took flesh, and God when He

---

[74] Jn. 10:30.   [75] Jn. 14:11.   [76] Jn. 14:9.

took flesh ... But there is danger that we think of Him in abstractions, not realizing the double principle of His headship and ascribing to Him a divided wisdom. We would then glorify a mutilated Christ. How is it possible to divide Christ in this way, when we must worship both His divinity and His flesh? Do we divide Him when we venerate the divine image and the cross at the same time? God forbid!

St. Cyril, bishop of Jerusalem, from the twelfth catechetical instruction:

Therefore, if you seek the reason for Christ's coming, go back to the beginning of Scripture. God created the world in six days, but the world was made for men. The sun is most radiant and brilliant, but we say that it was made for men. All living creatures were created to serve us; trees and flowers to give us joy. He called all creation good, but only men were made in His image. The sun came into existence by only a command, but man was fashioned by His own divine hands. "Let us make man in Our image, after Our likeness." If the wooden image of an earthly king is honored, how much more the reason-endowed image of God?

St. Gregory of Nazianzus, on baptism:

If after baptism the persecutor and tempter of the light assail you (for he assailed even the Word my God through the flesh by which the hidden light was revealed), you have the means to conquer him. Do not fear the conflict; defend yourself with the water; defend yourself with the Spirit. Rely on the seal and say to him "I myself am the image of God; I have not been cast down from heavenly glory, as you were through your pride; I have put on Christ; I have been transformed into Christ by baptism; you must worship me!"

St. John Chrysostom, on the Maccabees:

One finds that the images of emperors are made not only with gold, or silver, or the most valuable or beautiful materials, but one may find the same forms and likenesses in base metals. The differences between kinds of matter does not affect the worthiness of the image, nor is the honor of a superior material diminished by partaking of an inferior substance. The royal image always exalts whatever is used to portray it. It is not made dim by matter, but accomplishes the glorification of what it has received.

The same, from the first book against Julian the Apostate:

What does this new Nebuchadnezzar want? He has shown himself to be no kinder to us than the Nebuchadnezzar of old, but his burning coals shall afflict us no longer, for we have escaped from the flames. Do not the shrines of the saints placed in the churches for the worship of the faithful, still bear the marks of his damage?

The same, on the baptismal font:

Just as when the images or statues of the emperor are sent out and borne in procession through the city, and rulers and people acclaim them with applause and reverence, not honoring the wood, or the painted picture, but the form of the emperor, so it is also with created things . . .

Severianus of Gabala, from his fourth homily on the cross:

. . . For if in the emperor's absence, his image fills his place, and rulers bow before it, festivals are held in its presence, princes salute it, and the people prostrate themselves, not looking at the wood, but at the likeness of the emperor which makes him present not in essence but by visible representation, how much more shall the image of the immortal King . . .

Jerome, priest of Jerusalem, on the Holy Trinity:

Since the Scriptures nowhere command us to bow before the cross, why then do we delight to venerate it? Our response to Jews, Gentiles, and all peoples who ask us this question, is as follows: You fools and slow of heart. Perhaps God overlooked that all the Gentiles who honored Him worshipped earthly things, the handiwork of men, in order that when the fullness of time came, they would not be able

*to accuse Christians concerning the veneration of the cross
and other images. Just as the Jews venerated the ark of the
covenant, and the two cherubim hammered from gold, and
the two tablets which Moses gave them, although they had
received no command to venerate or kiss them, so it is also
with Christians. We do not embrace the cross as our God,
but the position of our bodies shows what our souls sincerely feel toward Him who was crucified.*

Simeon the Great, of the Mountain of Wonders, concerning images:

*Perhaps some contentious unbeliever might dispute with
us, saying that we venerate images in our churches, and he
had therefore concluded that we pray to lifeless idols. Far
be it from us to do this! Christians live by faith, and God,
who does not deceive us, has shown mighty signs in our
midst. Our images are not merely colored pictures; for when
we remember whose representation the painting is, we see
the invisible made visible through the visible representation,
and glorify Him who is made present, for we do not believe
in a God who is absent, but in Him who is truly present:
It is the same for the saints; they have not ceased to exist,
but they are present, because they are alive in God, and the
spirits of the saints are enabled by the power of God to help
those who pray to them.*

Anastasius, archbishop of Antioch, to Simeon, bishop
of Bostra, from the third oration:

*It is fitting for someone to bow before the emperor's
image because he wishes to honor the emperor, for the
image by itself is merely wax and paint.*

St. Anastasius of Mount Sinai, concerning the Lord's
Day and St. Thomas:

*Those who saw Christ in the flesh regarded Him as a
prophet. We, who have not seen Him, have confessed Him
from our youth and childhood as the Almighty and all-
powerful God, the Creator of the ages, and the radiance of
the Father. As if we saw Christ Himself speaking, we hear*

His Gospel with faith. We receive the most precious pearl of His Body, and presume that we have touched Christ Himself. And if we see only the image of His divine form, as if He were looking down upon us from heaven, we prostrate ourselves in veneration. Truly great is the Christian faith.

From the life of St. Mary of Egypt:

. . . And so I stood weeping when I saw above me the icon of the most holy Theotokos, and I prayed to her, "O Lady, Virgin and Theotokos, who gave birth in the flesh to God the Word, I know — how well I know! — that it is no honor or praise to you when someone so impure and depraved as I am looks upon your pure icon, for you kept your body and soul in purity, O ever-virgin. Before your virginal purity it is right that I inspire only hatred and disgust. But I have heard that God, who was born of you, became man only because He wanted to call sinners to repentance. Help me, for I have no other help! Order the entrance of the church to be opened to me. Allow me to see the venerable tree on which your Son suffered in the flesh and on which He shed His holy Blood for the redemption of sinners, and for me, unworthy as I am. Be my faithful witness before your Son that I will never again defile my body by fornication, but as soon as I see the tree of the cross I will renounce the world and its temptations and go wherever you lead me."

Thus I prayed and as if I obtained some hope in firm faith, and feeling some confidence in the mercy of the Theotokos, I left the place where I stood to pray. I went again and mingled with the crowd that was pushing its way into the church. And now no one seemed to thwart me; no one hindered my entering the church. I began to tremble, and was almost in a trance. Having got as far as the doors which I could not reach before — as if the same force which hindered me cleared the way for me — I now entered without any difficulty and found myself within the holy place. Throwing myself on the ground, I worshipped that holy earth and kissed it with trembling. Then I came out of the church and went to her who had promised to be my security, to the place where I made my vow. And bending my knees before the Virgin Theotokos, I prayed to her in words like these: "O loving Lady, you have shown me your great love for all men! Glory to God who receives the repentance of sinners through you."

From the life of St. Eupraxia:

. . . The deacon said to the maiden, "Leave your house, my child; it is not possible for you to remain here, for no one is able to stay here unless he is joined to Christ." The girl said to him "Where is Christ?" The deacon showed her an image of the Master, and she was converted in her heart; and said to the deacon: "Truly I unite myself to Christ; I will not leave my mistress." And Eupraxia rose up again and taking her maidservant, stood before the image of the Master, and raising her arms to heaven, she cried out with tears, "O Lord Jesus Christ, take care of this child, for she yearns for you; she commends herself to you."

From the life of the abbot Daniel, concerning Eulogius the quarryman:

. . . then he left the presence of the contemptuous man, and threw himself down before the icon of the Theotokos, and said with tears, "Lord, release me from the pledge I made this man!"

St. Methodius, bishop of the Patari, from his second sermon on the resurrection:

For example, even though the images of the emperor are not all made from gold or silver or precious metals, they are always honored by everyone. Men are not honoring the materials from which they are made; they do not choose to honor one image more than another because it is made from a more valuable substance; they honor the image whether it is made of cement or bronze. If you should mock any of them, you will not be judged differently for mocking plaster or gold; but for showing contempt to your king and lord. We make golden images of God's angels, principalities, and powers, to give glory and honor to Him.